D0351989

MEDIEVAL HOUSES OF WILTSHIRE

Publication of this book has been made possible through generous grants from:
The Marc Fitch Fund
Kennet District Council
Council for British Archaeology
The GWR Community Trust
and through a loan from the
Wiltshire Archaeological and Natural History Society

Plans

Plans are drawn to the scale 1:250 except where stated and direct comparison of sizes is possible. The scale line beneath each plan is divided into metres and the north point is shown. Following the usual convention, the front of the house is towards the bottom of the page.

Plans show the buildings at ground-floor level. They indicate as far as possible the early forms of the houses and most later extensions and alterations are omitted. Staircases are indicated by arrows, and former partitions and walls by dotted lines.

Key to rooms: H hall, IR inner room, P parlour, S service, B brewhouse, K kitchen, CP cross-passage, W well house, G garderobe.

Publications

In the text the Wiltshire Archaeological and Natural History Magazine is referred to as WAM and the magazine of the Vernacular Architecture Group as VA.

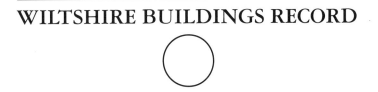

WILTSHIRE BUILDINGS RECORD

MEDIEVAL HOUSES OF WILTSHIRE

Pamela M. Slocombe

ALAN SUTTON

Monograph 3 in a series of selections from the Wiltshire Buildings Record archives

First published in the United Kingdom in 1992 by
Alan Sutton Publishing Ltd
Phoenix Mill · Far Thrupp · Stroud · Gloucestershire

First published in the United States of America in 1992 by
Alan Sutton Publishing Inc
83 Washington Street · Dover NH 03820

Copyright © Pamela Slocombe & Wiltshire Buildings Record
1992

All rights reserved. No part of this publication may be reproduced,
stored in a retrieval system, or transmitted, in any form, or by any
means, electronic, mechanical, photocopying, recording or
otherwise, without the prior permission of the publishers and
copyright holders.

Also available by the same author:
Wiltshire Farmhouses and Cottages 1500–1850
Wiltshire Farm Buildings 1500–1900

Titles in preparation include:
Town Houses of Wiltshire
Industrial Buildings of Wiltshire

British Cataloguing in Publication Data.

A Catalogue record for this book is available from the British
Library.

ISBN 0–7509–0285–X

Front cover: Watercolour of Talboys, Keevil, by W.W. Wheatley,
c. 1840. By kind permission of Mrs E.C. Crawford.

Typeset in 10/12pt Garamond.
Typesetting and origination by
Alan Sutton Publishing Limited.
Printed in Great Britain by
The Bath Press, Avon.

Foreword

Wiltshire is a county rich in prehistoric monuments – the world-famous sites of Stonehenge and Avebury have been studied since the seventeenth century and are merely the most impressive of a very rich record of early sites and structures.

By contrast the medieval period in the county has received far less attention. Without its prehistoric heritage, Wiltshire would be seen as a richly endowed county of medieval sites and these would have been studied and researched to the same extent as those in such counties as Somerset and Yorkshire. With such masterpieces as Salisbury Cathedral and sites of such national importance as Clarendon, there is clearly much of interest representing this period.

This book goes a long way towards remedying the lack of attention to the medieval heritage of Wiltshire in the past. Not only does it look at the greater monuments, the castles and abbeys, but the peasant-settlements, deserted villages and houses are also included. Most of the book looks at the vernacular architecture of the county for the medieval period – the first time this has been done.

This volume, together with the others in this series, will surely draw attention to the rich medieval heritage of Wiltshire and lead, I hope, to further research into the many features still so visible in the landscape of the county.

Michael Aston BA FSA MIFA,
Reader in Archaeology,
Department for Continuing Education,
University of Bristol

John Buckler's north view of the Red Lion Inn, Corsham, in 1809, showing an oriel window and a circular chimney with louvred top. By the early fifteenth century this was a house with one yardland in the hands of the Nott family and known as Winters Court. The Methuen Arms now occupies the site.

Introduction

It is not generally realized how widespread the remains of medieval houses are in England. They frequently hide, inconspicuous and unknown, behind later facades or isolated in the countryside.

This book goes back beyond the period covered by *Wiltshire Farmhouses and Cottages 1500–1850* (Wiltshire Buildings Record, 1988) to consider the houses of the Middle Ages, that is from the Norman Conquest in 1066 to around 1500. Little remains from the earliest part of this period, before 1200, but some indications of what there was can be gleaned from excavations and documents.

The aim of this book, and of the series, is to help people to identify and date features for themselves. Some technicalities, especially those of roof structures, are therefore included.

When trying to sort out the phases of development of a medieval building which has stood for so many centuries, readers should bear in mind the possibility that there may be seveal phases dating from before 1500. As we see today, a new generation or a new family coming to occupy a house almost always finds something to be repaired or improved.

Most of the buildings that are mentioned have been examined by members of the Wiltshire Buildings Record, but details of some are known only through the work of the Royal Commission on Historical Monuments, the National Trust or others.

Although the subject is primarily houses, some of the outbuildings with living quarters associated with large medieval houses are included. Medieval farm buildings also survive in Wiltshire. Details of about thirty-two barns are known, twenty-six of them still surviving. There are also dovecotes, a granary and possible byres and stables. None of these is covered here but some of their features are referred to where they help in the understanding of houses, which are often much more altered or difficult to examine.

Wiltshire in the Medieval Period

Though largely rural, Wiltshire already had ten boroughs in 1086. Wilton had been a regional capital, possibly with a castle, in the Saxon period. Early monasteries had been founded at Malmesbury and Bradford-on-Avon in the seventh and eighth centuries and at Old Sarum and Cricklade. Calne was also one of the early towns. Settlements were chiefly in the river valleys and the cultivated land was organized in manors. The rest of the country was forested or open downland already used for grazing sheep to produce wool. The population was quite small and ranked tenth among English counties in this respect. After the Norman Conquest in 1066, the Anglo-Saxon people suffered occupation by the Norman French and the county was militarized – dominated and controlled by troops garrisoned in the new castles that were being constructed. The larger of these were built by the king and the greater barons. Ludgershall Castle was built and at the end of the century the Bishop of Salisbury built a timber castle at Devizes. In 1086, William the Conqueror's court met at Lacock, suggesting that there was a hunting lodge or palace there. The town and castle of Old Sarum were flourishing from about 1075–8 onwards until the early thirteenth century. In August 1086, William received the Domesday records at Old Sarum and the homage of all his English vassals. The smaller castles were no more than fortified houses, and presumably the everyday lives of the country people and the houses they built remained largely unchanged.

The twelfth century

The next century saw the founding of various new monastic sites in Wiltshire. Monkton Farleigh Priory was founded in 1125, Bradenstoke in 1142, Ogbourne Priory in about 1149 and Maiden Bradley Priory in 1190. Malmesbury Abbey Church was rebuilt in about 1160–70. Many parish churches were built in the Romanesque style and a large number of stone fragments survive, especially of fonts and doorways where the best stone was used. Nikolaus Pevsner has said that about sixty of each still exist. By 1130 at least there was a royal palace at Clarendon. The building of castles continued and they were still used to plunder and control territory. In the early twelfth century, Trowbridge Castle was built. In 1118 the Bishop of Salisbury built a castle at Malmesbury, the men of which by 1140 were said to be exhausting the whole neighbourhood by their ravages. The Bishop's castle at Devizes which was burnt in 1113 was much rebuilt in 1120 and became of great importance. The associated St John's Church is one of the best Romanesque buildings surviving in the county. In 1137, Henry of Blois, Bishop of Winchester and brother of the king, built a motte and bailey castle at Downton. Calne Castle was possibly built at this time, and by 1175 there was a royal castle of stone at Marlborough, which remained in use till the mid-fourteenth century. A small textile industry was already established in the towns and the first fulling mills were built at the end of the century. The price of grain and other agricultural produce rose, leading to an expansion of cultivated land.

The thirteenth century

In the thirteenth century there were still large forests in the county and some house sites were established for verderers and others. Hunting was popular and deer parks were being created by the end of the century. This was the time when the largest number of moated sites were constructed in England. There were many water mills and a few windmills (an innovation of the end of the twelfth century). Another castle was constructed, at Mere in 1253. The manor houses of the county had gardens and, from around 1250 onwards, many had free-standing dovecotes. Monastic estates increased in general during the century. Between 1260 and 1296, William of Colerne, Abbot of Malmesbury, embarked on a huge programme of improving and consolidating the abbey's land holdings and repairing or replacing buildings. In 1218–19 the Bishop of Winchester built a new house for his manor of Fonthill, reroofing the barn. He also erected new buildings at East Knoyle and rethatched his barns, cowhouse and stables. In 1235 he retiled the great hall and garderobe at Downton and in 1251 erected a new barn there. From the beginning of the century, sheep and wool had become a large-scale and well-organized trade. Some individual tenants also had flocks and were able to buy some independence from the feudal system. The financial importance of markets encouraged land-owners to speculate by setting up new towns. The Bishop of Winchester founded 'the borough' at Downton in about 1205 and a town at Hindon between 1220 and 1250. Sherston was started at the beginning of the thirteenth century and Salisbury from the 1220s. Lacock Abbey was set up in 1229 and the town was started before 1247, with more development in 1285.

The fourteenth century

By the fourteenth century, Wiltshire was still the tenth county for population but it was now fourth (behind only Norfolk, Kent and Gloucestershire) for the amount of taxes raised, due to its good farmland, woollen trade and cloth industry. Salisbury became one of the leading cities of England, being in 1334 the ninth wealthiest provincial town and in 1377 the sixth largest provincial town in population. The interest in parks and hunting continued. In England in general, large numbers of moated sites were still being constructed in the early part of the century. The healthy economic situation was disrupted by the Black Death which seriously affected Wiltshire in 1348–9. Much land was neglected due to the deaths of tenants in the second half of the century, and surviving landowners greatly increased their holdings by purchasing, probably at low prices, the lands of families that had been affected. Building activity was low during the Black Death period but increased from the 1370s onwards. In the 1390s, Thomas Calston was rebuilding Bewley Court at Lacock and in about 1393 Wardour Castle was begun.

The fifteenth century

In the late medieval period before 1550, Wiltshire, because of the cloth trade, was in the second wealthiest area of England. This was an L-shaped region including Dorset, Hampshire and Sussex, and running North to Worcestershire. The wealthiest areas were the South-west – Cornwall, Devon and Somerset – and parts of the east of England – Kent, Surrey, Essex, Suffolk, Middlesex and Cambridgeshire. About half of the houses at Castle Combe, a small cloth town, were built or rebuilt in the first half of the fifteenth century. Many merchants' houses were built at Salisbury and to a lesser extent in other towns like Trowbridge. Religion was very important and many chantries were founded. This was the final flowering of the monastic estates which were highly organized. Many of the surviving houses of cruck construction were on these estates. A larger number of both urban and rural buildings survive from the fifteenth century than from previous centuries.

Types of settlement

Some of the very oldest farm sites originated as groups of two or three dwellings isolated in the countryside, as explained in *Wiltshire Farm Buildings 1500–1900* (Wiltshire Buildings Record, 1989). In the medieval period the county also had quite a high density of larger settlement sites of village or hamlet size in the river valleys and lower land. The downland has never been suitable for intensive cultivation and settlement. In west Wiltshire in the triangle between Warminster, Chippenham and Devizes, the density of sites was especially high compared with any area of England, and this has not been satisfactorily explained. It may perhaps be connected with the woollen industry and the suitability of the rivers for mills. Many of these settlements, often only a mile or so apart, were abandoned when economic conditions changed and became what are now known as deserted or shrunken medieval villages. A number of surviving, isolated medieval manor houses, like Sheldon Manor in Chippenham Without, originated in this way.

On the slopes of the downland areas there are a number of long, thin parishes. The main settlement is on the spring line and the parish has a share of hillside arable land, valley pasture and extensive downland grazing. This was the most efficient way of using the downland, as part of a larger agricultural system. Examples of these villages are readily visible on a map, especially in the Shrewton and Rushall areas.
Wiltshire has a number of settlements that were deliberately 'planted' in the medieval period and which still display this in the

pattern of their streets and roads. These were speculative developments by large ecclesiastical or lay estates and usually contain a wide market place where it was hoped the money would be made. Some of the towns have fan-shaped street systems at the foot of a castle mound, such as Devizes and Trowbridge. Some have a fairly square grid pattern, such as Salisbury and Lacock. Some have chiefly a long, wide street acting as a market place, such as Marlborough and Hindon. Some villages also show signs of plots having been laid out regularly at some date. The name, Row, is sometimes used for a series of house plots in a line, for example Seend Row at Seend. Other settlements, such as the hamlet of Heddington Wick in Heddington parish, Biddestone and Poulshot, have houses grouped around a communal green. This type is especially common in areas of former woodland. Nucleated villages, tightly clustered around a church and manor-house, also exist in the county. These developed in the medieval rather than the Saxon period.

Castles and royal manors

Wiltshire has the remains of very few castles today but there were many more in the medieval period. Some have already been mentioned. Another important castle was at Castle Combe. The Norman keep had walls about 3 m thick and the lower chamber in it measured 4.8 m by 3.7 m. It was the chief residence of the de Dunstanvilles, barons of Castle Combe, from the eleventh to the thirteenth centuries. Other castle sites exist at Great Bedwyn, Castle Eaton, Chippenham (possibly a Norman motte), Sherston and perhaps Sherrington.

There were large royal estates in the county, some of which were granted to favourites at different times and later taken back. The largest estates in the eleventh century and later were centred on Malmesbury, Chippenham, Corsham, Box, Melksham, Bradford-on-Avon, Devizes and Rowde, Marlborough, Clarendon and Old Sarum. Other royal manors were at Lydiard Millicent, Calne, Bromham, Warminster, Westbury and East Knoyle in the north and west of the county, and at Bedwyn, Wootton Rivers, Collingbourne Ducis and Amesbury in the east. Bradford-on-Avon was granted by the king to Shaftesbury Abbey in 1001, and Devizes and Rowde only came into royal hands when Devizes Castle was seized from the Bishop of Salisbury in 1139. There was a royal palace at Clarendon by 1130 or earlier which was in ruins in the thirteenth century but much used in the fourteenth and until the end of the fifteenth centuries. The royal lands were extensively forested and were used for hunting, so there were also royal hunting lodges.

Boroughs and towns

Jeremy Haslam's book, *Wiltshire Towns*, describes twenty-nine settlements that had town status in the Middle Ages. Some failed to develop and are now considered to be villages, such as Great Bedwyn, Heytesbury, Lacock, Market Lavington, Ramsbury and Tilshead. Others could perhaps be added to the list such as Steeple Ashton, which was granted a weekly market and a yearly three-day fair in 1266, and Upavon, which had markets and fairs from the thirteenth century onwards.

Aldbourne and Potterne also had considerably more status in their areas than they have today.

Monasteries and other ecclesiastical estates

Before the Norman Conquest there were already extensive monastic estates in Wiltshire, and in the next few centuries these were greatly increased by new foundations and gifts of land. By the time of the Dissolution in the 1530s a very considerable proportion of the county was in ecclesiastical hands.

Forty-nine ecclesiastical establishments are listed in the *Victoria County History of Wiltshire* (*fig. 1*). These cluster especially around Salisbury and Marlborough, but with others dotted all over the county and particularly in a band from Wootton Bassett to Bradford-on-Avon, linked to the rich pasture lands of the River Avon and its tributaries.

A map of the position of the religious houses (*fig. 1*) gives only part of the picture; it does not show the extent of the manors and lands held by each house. It also gives no indication of the holdings of other houses situated outside the county. For example, according to C.J. Bond and J.B. Weller, Glastonbury Abbey in Somerset by 1086 already held 258 hides of land in fourteen named vills in Wiltshire. Shaftesbury Abbey in Dorset had very large estates, especially the huge manor of Bradford-on-Avon and that of Tisbury. Romsey Abbey in Hampshire held the equally large manor of Steeple Ashton. Other houses with lands, outside of the county, included Winchester, Westminster, Battle, Keynsham, Cirencester and Hinton in Somerset.

Religious holdings are often reflected in place-names, such as Monkton in Broughton Gifford which was an estate of the Prior of Monkton Farleigh. The hamlet, Temple at Corsley, and Temple Farm at Rockley, Ogbourne St Andrew belonged to the Knights Templar. Bishop's Cannings belonged to the Bishop of Salisbury and Bishopstone, southwest of Salisbury, was a living of the bishops of Winchester.

Many of the sites of religious houses have some of the medieval domestic and service buildings surviving today, often in a very disguised form. Some are well known and some have been discovered in recent years during fieldwork for the Wiltshire Buildings Record. Discoveries include Clatford Hall, Preshute which retains the thick, stone walls, a roof truss and re-used moulded ceiling timbers from the alien house there. Another is Old Abbey Farmhouse, Stanley, Calne Without (*back cover*) which is remodelled from one of the buildings of Stanley Abbey, and has thick walls and a smoke-blackened roof. Other examples of remains, some well known, are: Lacock Abbey; Wilton House (with a recently discovered doorway from the time of Wilton Abbey); Edington Priory; Priory Farmhouse, Kington St Michael; Longleat (said to incorporate some fragments of St Radegund's Priory); Maiden Bradley Priory (now farm buildings); Abbey House; the Bell Inn and brewery buildings, Malmesbury; and buildings at Bradenstoke. Features

Key to Ecclesiastical Map

SECULAR CANONS
1. Salisbury Cathedral

BENEDICTINE MONKS
2. Malmesbury Abbey

BENEDICTINE NUNS
3. Wilton Abbey
4. Amesbury Abbey, later Priory
5. Kington St. Michael Priory

CLUNIAC MONKS
6. Monkton Farleigh Priory

CISTERCIAN MONKS
7. Stanley Abbey

AUGUSTINIAN CANONS
8. Bradenstoke Priory
9. Ivychurch Priory
10. Maiden Bradley Priory
11. Longleat Priory

AUGUSTINIAN CANONESSES
12. Lacock Abbey

GILBERTINE CANONS
13. Marlborough Priory
14. Poulton Priory

BONHOMMES
15. Edington

TRINITARIANS
16. Easton Priory or Hospital

KNIGHTS TEMPLARS
17. Temple Rockley Preceptory

KNIGHTS HOSPITALLERS
18. Ansty Preceptory

FRIARS
19. Salisbury Franciscan
20. Wilton Dominican

21. Salisbury Dominican
22. Marlborough Carmelite

HOSPITALS
23. Great Bedwyn, St John the Baptist
24. Bradford-on-Avon, St Margaret
25. Calne, St John the Baptist and St Anthony
26. Cricklade, St John the Baptist
27. Devizes, St John the Baptist
28. Heytesbury, St John and St Katherine
29. Malmesbury, St John the Baptist
30. Malmesbury, St Mary Magdalene
31. Marlborough, St John the Baptist
32. Marlborough, St Thomas the Martyr
33. Salisbury, Holy Trinity
35. Salisbury, St John the Baptist and St Anthony
36. Southbroom, St James and St Denis
37. Wilton, St Giles and St Anthony
38. Wilton, St John the Baptist
39. Wilton, St Mary Magdalene
40. Wootton Bassett, St John the Baptist

COLLEGES
41. Salisbury, De Vaux
42. Salisbury, St Edmund
43. Heytesbury, St Peter and St Paul

ALIEN HOUSES
44. Avebury Priory
45. Charlton Priory
46. Clatford Priory
47. Corsham Priory
48. Ogbourne Priory
49. Upavon Priory

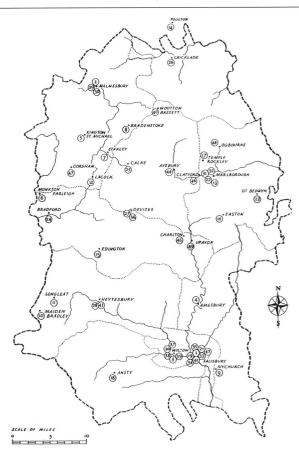

Fig. 1 Map of Wiltshire showing the religious houses. The boundaries are the rural deaneries in 1535. Reproduced with permission from the 'Victoria County History of Wiltshire', Vol. 3.

13

of some of these buildings are illustrated later in this book. Many other survivals could be quoted for Salisbury and elsewhere.

The influence of the religious houses on architecture is also felt throughout their estates. The manor houses, especially those of granges, were very well built. They often had rooms for officials managing the estate and a wing with special quarters for the steward or for visits by the head of the order, frequently in the form of a solar or great chamber on the first floor. Usually these houses seem from descriptions to have been larger in the medieval period than now and to have lost wings or closely adjoining buildings when they declined in status at the Dissolution or later. Examples of such manor houses are Barton Farm, Bradford-on-Avon; Place Farm (originally called Hall Place), Tisbury; Garsdon Manor, Lea and Cleverton; Cloatley Manor, Hankerton; and Fowlswick Farm, Chippenham Without. The last three belonged to Malmesbury Abbey.

Some domestic ecclesiastical buildings are only known from excavation, such as the Bishop's Palace at Potterne which dated from at least the late thirteenth century. At Salisbury the canons' houses in the Close form a compact group of high status ecclesiastical houses with many early features from the thirteenth century onwards. Farmhouses and cottages on ecclesiastical estates seem to be especially well built too. The incidence of cruck buildings there is discussed later (pp.79–80).

The larger monasteries of the Middle Ages should be seen as huge business enterprises with sufficient resources to be able to turn to any industrial or agricultural line that was profitable. In Wiltshire, sheep, wool and cloth-making were the main source of income and large flocks were kept on the downs. Excavated houses at Fyfield are thought to have been a specially constructed settlement for sheep farming, similar to the bercaries in Yorkshire. Mills were built in the river valleys for fulling the cloth. Other large-scale agricultural enterprises were corn growing (resulting, along with the collection of tithes, in enormous barns), the huge dovecotes of the manor houses, the fisheries and the specialized dairy farms or wicks. The ecclesiastical landlords were also involved in stone quarrying and potteries. Glastonbury Abbey owned the potteries at Crockerton, Longbridge Deverill, and the Bishop of Salisbury had those at Potterne. Stanley Abbey was digging iron ore in the thirteenth century. Many of the manor houses were sited close to these valuable assets to control them.

University college estates

The universities were also originally religious institutions. Oxford University was near enough to acquire some estates in Wiltshire in the Middle Ages. New College, set up in 1379 and the first college to admit undergraduates, was given the manor of Colerne by the Bishop of Winchester subject to a life interest which was bought out in 1389. Its accounts for the manor start in 1393. The college also acquired estates in Alton Barnes and Stert. Magdalen College had property in Market Lavington before the Dissolution. At Cambridge University, in existence by 1229, King's College had the rectory estates of Broad Chalke, Bower Chalke and Alvediston from 1448 onwards.

Lay magnates

Apart from the large institutional owners there were also great families who owned estates in the county. Some held one or more manors and some had freehold estates within manors. The wealthiest people were those who had a national role as well as a local one, with perhaps a well-paid position at court. Their wealth is reflected in the quality of their houses.

An early example is Adam de Stratton, a royal official who had estates around Highworth in the thirteenth century.

Thomas Rogers, sergeant-at-law (a high-ranking barrister by royal appointment), built (or remodelled) the house later called the Priory at Bradford-on-Avon in about 1460. He acquired the property through his wife Cecilia Besill.

Another example, mentioned later (p. 17), is the Croke family of Wick Farm, Lacock, and Hazelbury Manor, Box, who were also linked with Fowlswick Farm, Chippenham Without. Reginald Croke of Wick, who died in 1297, was a county coroner and may have been attached to the royal household.

Thomas Calston of Bewley Court, Lacock, could claim descent from Henry II through his grandmother. He held numerous offices, including Commissioner of Array (gathering troops) in 1399, 1402 and 1403, escheator for Wiltshire and Hampshire, and High Sheriff of Wiltshire, representing the king. Calston's property also included Littlecote House, Ramsbury.

The Pavelys of Brook Hall, Heywood and Dauntsey Manor, Dauntsey, were an important family with many retainers. Walter de Pavely, lord of Westbury in 1315, was twice a member of parliament for Wiltshire in 1313. He may have rebuilt Dauntsey Manor, a large base-cruck hall house. Brook was rebuilt in the late fifteenth century.

Thomas Tropenell, who built Great Chalfield, was in 1429 MP for Bedwyn, a pocket borough of the Hungerford family for whom he was steward. Later, once or twice, he was MP for Bath.

There were also prominent families in the towns. Members of Parliament's houses include the Hall of John Hall at Salisbury. Hall was an MP and several times Mayor of Salisbury between 1450 and 1461.

There is some evidence that Great Porch at Devizes was a house of the Coventry family who were merchants and also mayors and MPs for Devizes. The Coventrys oversaw work for Queen Joan of Navarre in the town, and the carved head of her husband, Henry IV, is in the house. The only fifteenth-century stone house in the town, 4 St John's Court, was certainly one of their other houses.

From the fifteenth century onwards, younger sons of good families who made money in the cloth trade became more important, and built good houses or acquired houses already built by the gentry or the Church. William Brent and, later, Thomas Barkesdale, both clothiers, lived at Talboys, Keevil, in the late fifteenth century (*front cover*).

The house that is traditionally said to have been Maud Heath's at Langley Green, Langley Burrell Without, was a well-made but simple cruck house of three-room and cross-passage plan, yet she was able to leave extensive property in her will to endow a causeway to Chippenham. Before the sixteenth century, the clothiers mostly had leasehold land within manors and had to wait until the Dissolution to gain control of some of the prime house sites and lands in the county. In the towns, other tradesmen with considerable wealth included grocers (i.e. wholesalers) and goldsmiths.

The forests

In Neolithic times, 80 per cent of the countryside was still forested but this proportion was gradually reduced over the centuries for the benefit of ploughing and grazing. By 1086 about 15 per cent of the land is thought to have been still wooded. After the Conquest the Normans took a greater interest in the remaining forest areas and actively set aside lands to be subject to forest law. In the eleventh century, Wiltshire already had extensive forests, created in the well-wooded and therefore less-settled areas of the county, based on royal manors but extending beyond them. By the thirteenth century there were four royal forests in the western half of Wiltshire – Braydon, Chippenham, Melksham and Selwood – and five forests in the eastern half – Savernake, Chute, Clarendon, Melchet and Grovely. The four western forests were detached portions left from what had been the very large forest of Selwood in the Saxon period.

The main motive for the maintenance of the forests was hunting, the favourite royal pastime, for which large herds of deer were kept. The timber was of great economic importance for building and firewood and a number of other enterprises were linked to the wood/pasture economy including the keeping of large herds of swine, dairying and fish-ponds. To control the deer, parks were established. Oliver Rackham has estimated that there were 3,200 deer parks in England in 1300. There were leap gates into the parks (giving Lypiatt place-names), and it was necessary to dig ditches on low land or plant thick hedges on higher land round pasture fields. One of the reasons why moats were put round larger houses and gardens was to exclude the deer. Many isolated farms still have a 'park' name today, for example in the centre of the county, Potterne Park Farm, a moated site, Seend Park Farm and Melksham Park Farm. At Bewley Court, Lacock (ley and leigh names usually indicate clearings), there were medieval ditched fields, and the house probably had a fish-pond and a moat.

The forest areas were subject to very severe forest law and had to be well patrolled to combat poaching. When hunting took place a lodge was needed as a base. People were needed to assist with hunting and in addition there were many occupations connected with the timber industry. All of this led to houses in the forests. Clarendon Palace is thought to have originated as a hunting lodge in the eleventh century. King John issued documents from Cherhill in Chippenham Forest which suggests there was a hunting lodge there. Rushmore House is thought to be on the site of a medieval lodge in Cranbourne Chase.

The dairying element of the wood-pasture economy survived the eventual loss of the forests in north and west Wiltshire and reached its high point in the eighteenth century. In the medieval period, many 'wicks' or dairy farms had been set up. Several were linked to the Croke family who were probably of Norman origin. From the late eleventh century until 1482, when the direct male line became extinct, the family held a number of Wiltshire manors. They had hereditary offices as huntsmen or other forest officials and there were branches of the family in Wiltshire, Hampshire and Staffordshire. In 1130–1131, Ruald Croc was in charge of seven dairy farms in the New Forest, each with twenty cows and a bull. In Wiltshire they were at Hazelbury, Box; Wick Farm, Lacock which had fish-ponds; and Fowlswick, Chippenham Without, a moated site. One of a number of moated sites in west Wiltshire has a 'wick' name: Southwick Court at Southwick.

Population pressures on land, the demand for timber and the decline of hunting were some of the factors that led gradually to the clearing of much of the forests and the final removal of forest law. The effect of the forests is still, however, visible in the place-names of Wiltshire and explains many isolated early house sites.

Archaeological Evidence

Until recent years, few complete medieval settlements had been excavated in England. It was the general belief that medieval peasant houses were poorly built, lasting only a generation. This view is now being modified in the light of excavations at Wharram Percy in Yorkshire and elsewhere.

Excavations in Wiltshire have contributed to a knowledge of the royal palace at Clarendon and the domestic quarters of the main castles. A part of the Bishop's Palace at Potterne was uncovered in 1973 (WAM 69). Excavations of sites below that social level have been fairly few. The Anglo-Saxon starting point is provided by sites such as Cowage Farm, Foxley, Norton, where excavations in about 1980 by John Hinchcliffe and aerial photography by the Royal Commission on the Historical Monuments of England have revealed a timber hall with narrow, partitioned sections at each end. Excavations by the County Council at Swindon uncovered Anglo-Saxon buildings with sunken floors, and stud walls infilled with wattle and daub, which were probably weaving huts.

Early medieval features found in excavations in other counties include earth-fast posts (set directly into the ground), the use of timbers of small section with multiple bracing, scissor-bracing and walling with vertical planks. Plans include boat-shaped and aisled buildings. Boat-shaped plans were used in the fifth to tenth centuries in Scandinavia, northern Germany, the Netherlands and England.

H.C. Bowen and P.J. Fowler excavated the hamlet of Raddon, Fyfield, as part of a study of Fyfield and Overton Downs, near Marlborough, begun in 1959. They found houses dating from the first half of the twelfth century until about 1300 (WAM 58). The settlement was a bercary or sheep farm belonging to the prior of St Swithun's at Winchester. There were longhouses and a possible aisled building. The houses had low sarsen walls, one or two courses high and about 0.9 m thick, and were presumably timber-framed above. One building had central posts and another was boat-shaped.

Between 1963 and 1968, Musty and Algar carried out excavations at Gomeldon, Idmiston, a similar downland sheep and arable holding. In this case belonging to Glastonbury Abbey in Somerset. They discovered a building of the late twelfth century and a number of buildings of the thirteenth and fourteenth centuries. The twelfth-century building (WAM 80, p. 148) was a longhouse with earth-fast cruck timbers. Its plan included a living room, a cross passage, and a byre at one end confirmed by the presence of a drain. The corners of the building were rounded. The complex developed so that by the end of the thirteenth century there was a yard and a barn. Bones showed that sheep were the main animal kept there, with oxen for ploughing and other work.

Medieval house sites occupied from the eleventh to the fourteenth centuries near the church at Huish were excavated by N.P. Thompson (WAM 62 and 63). One building, possibly a barn, had in its fifteenth-century phase, foundations walls of small chalk rubble up to 0.3 m high and 0.6 m wide. Externally it measured 8.5 m by 4.9 m. Earlier phases of the same building were represented by post-holes, some containing eleventh-century pottery and five large sarsen boulders. This suggests the usual sequence of earth-fast posts, then the feet of the timbers set up on boulders and, finally, low walls supporting the timber-framed structure.

At Littlecote, Ramsbury, a medieval settlement abandoned in about 1450 was excavated from 1984 onwards. B. Phillips reported a flint-walled longhouse built in about 1250 (Medieval Village Research Group, Annual Report, 1985). It had a living area with a hearth and traces of an oven, a chamber, a cobbled cross-passage and a chalk-floored byre. Nearby was a barn apparently of timber-framing over low, flint-based walls. Another house, associated with iron-working, was of timber construction with posts either set into the ground or resting on flints. It was replaced by a three-roomed longhouse with a cob living end and a flint-walled byre. The living end was later built of timber posts set on sarsens. At Raddon, Gomeldon and Littlecote there were large ovens near the buildings which may have been corn-drying kilns.

Dating Methods

The accurate dating of medieval houses and their features can be difficult as inscribed dates are rare and documentary evidence is sparser than for later buildings. However, there are sometimes clues. At Talboys, Keevil, a coat of arms painted on the gallery is of 1432 or later (*no. 1*). At the Hall of John Hall, Salisbury, a shield of arms and a merchant's mark on a fireplace indicate the owner. When John Aubrey was looking at medieval houses in the seventeenth century there was a great deal of early window glass with coats of arms and inscriptions surviving. Very little remains now but he recorded much of what he saw.

At Hemingsby, a house in the Close at Salisbury, a cornice in the hall has the inscription, 'W. Fideon', commemorating Canon Fideon who altered it between 1457 and 1474. In such cases the decision still needs to be made as to what he altered and how far he rebuilt.

Lesser houses are usually harder to date as they are less likely to have such details, or, in fact, much decoration at all. It may only be possible to put a wide date bracket such as 1350–1450 using similarities of construction, carpentry methods and so on, compared with other more datable houses. It is difficult in Wiltshire to distinguish between houses of the late fifteenth century and those of

No. 1 The hall gallery at Talboys, Keevil, with the arms of Arundel quartered with Maltravers surrounded by the garter, received in 1432. To the left is a possible merchant's mark. The house was formerly called Brent Place after the clothier William Brent and the Arundels were Lords of the Manor.

the first half of the sixteenth century. The latter period was illustrated in our first book, *Wiltshire Farmhouses and Cottages*. Some criteria for distinguishing between the two are now becoming clear and some houses previously assigned to the fifteenth century are now better placed in the sixteenth, filling a gap which had previously been recognized in the sequence of Wiltshire's building.

In recent years a more reliable method of dating houses, called dendrochronology or tree-ring dating, has been developed. The patterns of annual growth of wood from a particular tree are matched against a known local sequence of year growths. Annular rings vary with the rainfall. Where there is a good sample including some sapwood or even bark, this is an accurate way of telling which year and even which time of year a tree was felled. Timber was usually used shortly after felling. An English sequence, for oak only, now runs from AD 404 to the present, but the process can be quite costly as the matching is done by computer not by eye.

Very few Wiltshire buildings have so far been dendro-dated and it is obviously important to identify which phase of a building the sample is taken from, or a timber used in alteration or repair might be thought to give an original date. For example, forty timbers from Siddington tithe barn in Gloucestershire have been sampled, giving two dates: a construction date in or shortly after 1245–7 with alteration to the porches in the fifteenth century.

Wood can also be dated by the carbon-14 method which is less accurate. A small timber-framed house, 88–90 Chilton Foliat, was shown by this method to date from between 1390 and 1480, with alterations in 1580–1670.

Documentary Evidence

Many types of document can provide an insight into local medieval houses. Little survives from the eleventh and twelfth centuries, but the amount of information increases between the thirteenth and fifteenth centuries.

There are court cases, feet of fines (recording transfers of land and buildings), a few inventories listing people's personal possessions at death, some building contracts and accounts, monastic accounts and rentals, inquisitions post mortem (IPMs) recording people's land and buildings at death, surveys of manors, custumals (with rents, services and the customs of a manor), and eyewitness descriptions of buildings now long gone. Many early documents are in abbreviated Latin and very difficult to read without training, but the Wiltshire Record Society is gradually publishing transcriptions of some collections. Extracts can also be found in volumes of the *Victoria County History of Wiltshire* and elsewhere.

Some examples can be given to provide an idea of what exists:
The first, of about 1130, from the records of Shaftesbury Abbey, concerns Avoncliff Mill, Westwood, but illustrates the provision of timber for tenants. Godric, in return for his rent – 15 sticks of eels and a duty to plough and reap an acre – had an allocation of 'every year one tree in the wood and the help of men and carts to the broken mill and for carrying millstones'.

From the Crown pleas of the Wiltshire eyre in 1249:
Agnes of Lavinton was crushed by an old house in which she was lodged in Devizes. The deodand (forfeited instrument of death) was timber worth 18 d. Various court cases concern people burning down houses, for example unknown evildoers came by night to the house of Robert Edward of Latton, and burned the house and killed Simon, Robert's servant. There were also accidental burnings. At Tilshead a six-month-old boy was killed when a house burned down.

From the cartulary listing the deeds belonging to Edington Priory:
1225 at Lavington, a capital messuage, garden, mill which stands in front of its gate, stewpond and granary near the courtyard.
1329 the Lord of Keevil manor, the Earl of Arundel (died 1326) had the custom of providing the rector with thorns from his park for the repair of his house.
1395 the vicar of Keevil is to have the upper part (high end) of the rectory house. The rector and convent of Edington should put up the doors and gateways necessary in the vicarage house and are allowed to place their ladders on vicarage land to repair the walls between the rectory house and the vicarage house.

IPMs:
1350 Fifield Bavant, Ebbesbourne Wake. A hall, chamber, chapel roofed with stone. A kitchen, bakehouse and brewhouse in ruinous state. Oxhouse, stable and all other houses except the grange {barn} ruinous. Ruinous dovecote.

A tiny church, probably the former chapel, is now all that stands at this site.

In the fourteenth century the IPMs show that many manor houses were worth little or nothing. At Great Wishford the outhouses of a messuage were 'in a bad state and broken down'.

Accounts of Shaftesbury Abbey for Barton Farm, Bradford-on-Avon:

> 1392 carpenter taking down and mending old pentice over the well and making woodwork anew. 14 days.
>
> 2 masons mending walls of pentice. 2 days.
>
> Tiler tiling skilling round well and trough, with splitting and perforating slates. 15 days.

Extent of the Earl of Arundel's Keevil Manor 1397 (printed in Edith Rickert's *Chaucer's World*):

> A hall, a chief chamber, and a little chamber next thereunto with a latrine at the back of the same hall, roofed with tiles. A chamber below the said great chamber and another chamber and latrine next thereunto. A chapel and a cellar below the chapel. A chamber called 'le warderobe' likewise at the end of the hall, and the entrance thereof is a great chamber with a latrine, and below that chamber is a pantry and buttery. There is a great kitchen newly repaired. A long house called 'kyghtenchambre'. A house for the office of bakery and two chambers for grooms. A chamber beyond the gate with a latrine, entirely roofed with tiles. A long stable and a little stable and a barn partly roofed anew with straw in great need of repair. A dovecote and two gardens.

An IPM of 1327 reveals that at that date the chief messuage at Keevil and its outbuildings had been ruinous.

Inventories:

For the George Inn, Salisbury there is a list of goods and utensils of the deceased owner in 1410 when the building was a private house and a list of the permanent fittings in 1474 for a lease. In 1474 all the chambers of the inn had beds and tables but only one had a fireplace.

For Bewley Court, Lacock, in 1418 (WAM 81), an IPM lists all the rooms of the house and their numerous contents. Items in the hall include three tables with two trestles, a chair and six stools.

Building contracts and accounts:

Sheldon Manor in 1431. Work included the addition of the cross-wing, 'raising a chamber for walplates on the east side of the hall of Shulledon'. A carpenter was paid for propping up various members in the Treasury and a mason for repairing all defaults of stone walls of the house.

1444 Blue Boar Hall, rear of 41 Market Place, Salisbury (WAM 15). The contract was between William Ludlow, Lord of Hill Deverill and butler to Henry IV, and John Fayrebowe, a carpenter of Bishopstrow about 2½ miles from Hill Deverill. It specifies the overall size of the house and the sizes of individual timbers: groundsill, posts, beams, joists, etc. The timber was to be 'clene withoute sape or wyndshake'. The date by which it was to be erected was specified and the owner was to supply two men for seven days to help with the rearing of the house. Payment was to be in three stages: before the hewing of the wood, when the prepared timber was brought to Salisbury and when the house had been erected. The total carpenter's bill was £20.

Westwood Manor 1480. Thomas Culverhouse, the tenant, claimed £37 14s 5d from Winchester for building work. This included 120 cartloads of stone, 9000 stone tiles, 70 ft of crests, 148 sacks of lime, ironwork, and some labour, but not the timber involved, which may have been provided.

Surveys:
Castle Combe Manor. In about 1459, William of Worcester, the agent of Sir John Fastolf, listed the tenants, often with the house name, the street name or a location description, and he gave the rent payable. For example, under cottages an entry translates from Latin as 'Edith Lacock, widow of John Lacock, holds a tenement called Monday's thing, formerly held by Roger Batt in West Street, and pays annually 2s'. Mondaymen worked for the lord of the manor on Mondays.

Several people were ordered to repair their houses and a list was made of new building in the time of Sir John Fastolf, since 1409. Fifty houses and two mills were concerned. For example, William Ferron made and built his house anew of stone, Thomas Lane well repaired his tenement and John Rede and Cecilia Rede newly built four tenements of stone.

Descriptions:
Many houses are mentioned by Leland who visited Wiltshire in the mid-sixteenth century and by John Aubrey, the antiquarian who lived at Easton Percy in the late seventeenth century.

Pictorial evidence

John Aubrey's drawings of medieval buildings as they appeared in the seventeenth century are a very useful source, though the redrawings by Kite in Aubrey and Jackson are sometimes not altogether accurate. Other drawings that are useful but which cannot be assumed always to be in proportion are those of John Buckler (early nineteenth century), W.W. Wheatley (1811–1885) and J.H. Parker (mid-nineteenth century). About 700 of Buckler's drawings dating from 1803–11 are at Devizes Museum. They

Fig. 2 Woodlands Manor, Mere, drawn by P. Crocker and published in the **'Gentleman's Magazine'** *in August 1825.*

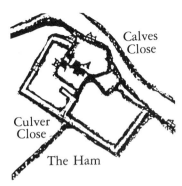

Calves Close

Culver Close

The Ham

Fig. 3 Fowlswick Farm, Chippenham Without, shown on an estate map of 1766 with the double moat clearly shown. A is the house and B a dovecote now gone.

sections of a house are sometimes shown, for example part of Woodlands Manor, Mere, in an 1825 drawing (*fig. 2*).

Old estate maps are a useful source of information and may reveal earlier plans of buildings and the sites of moats, fish-ponds and other features (*fig. 3*). For about 1860 onwards, photographs begin to be available. *No. 2* is one of Harold Brakspear's photographs of Bewley Court before alteration.

mostly show churches but there are often houses in the background, and a number feature houses, for example (*frontispiece*) the Red Lion Inn (rebuilt *c.* 1810) at Corsham and Porch House, Potterne (*c.* 1810) before its nineteenth century renovations. One of Wheatley's paintings is illustrated on the front cover. Many other old prints and architectural drawings by different artists and architects can be seen at the Devizes Museum Library, and in the photographic collection of the Wiltshire Library and Museum Service at Trowbridge. T.L. Walker's *Examples of Gothic Architecture* of 1838 has excellent plans, elevations, sections and details of the manor houses at South Wraxall and Great Chalfield.

From drawings of houses now altered or gone it is often possible to deduce the plan and functions of some of the rooms. Ruined

No. 2 South-west corner of the hall at Bewley Court, Lacock, showing the stone corbel supporting the roof truss, a moulded outline on the wall, the top of the archway leading to the staircase and the older timber-framed partition. Taken by Harold Brakspear in about 1912 before alterations.

Factors Affecting the Survival of Medieval Houses

Population estimates for the period 1066–1500 cannot be very accurate. It is thought that England as a whole had just under two million inhabitants in 1066, rising to over four million in the early fourteenth century, and dropping back to under three million after the Black Death before increasing again in the fifteenth century. Wiltshire probably reflected this pattern. Taxation lists give an indication of the number of households in a community at various dates, so the likely number of houses can be deduced. Market Lavington had 252 poll-tax payers in 1377, about as many as Chippenham. During much of the period many villages would have had fewer than ten houses.

In recent years, dating by dendrochronology in Oxfordshire has shown that parts of some timber houses from the twelfth or even the eleventh century can survive in Southern England. This must be rare but it would be surprising if in planted towns like Lacock and Salisbury nothing from the best houses of the original thirteenth-century settlement remained.

Most of the reasons for rebuilding throughout history can still be observed today. The earliest remains of building on a site may represent (a) development on a new site responding to population pressures; (b) a rebuilding following war, fire, storm damage or disease; (c) a new building technique available; (d) a change of plan or substantial enlargement from what preceded; (e) a new building material available; (f) the purchase of the site by a wealthy, improving landlord after a period of neglect or disputed ownership.

Many villages and towns become 'fossilized' with the houses retaining their appearance during the last period of great economic growth. Thus Salisbury retains today many houses of the fifteenth century and Steeple Ashton has a number still showing fifteenth and sixteenth-century features externally, but Trowbridge, Devizes and Bradford-on-Avon, though also flourishing medieval towns, have an eighteenth-century appearance due to the later success there of the woollen trade. However, behind the facades, the carcass of a house may still remain from the earlier period of prosperity.

Some towns and villages have few, if any, medieval buildings. Why does Mere have fewer than Lacock or Sherston fewer than Malmesbury? The wealth of the community and the quality of local building materials are important factors. Fires, the second cause for rebuilding given above, played a part in some cases. Recorded cases of damaging fires include Malmesbury (1042), Calne (1341, greater part of the best houses destroyed), Steeple Ashton (1503), Sherston (1511 'completely burnt'), Ramsbury (1648), Marlborough (1653, extensive damage in the High Street), Mere (1670, fifty-four houses burned), Netheravon (1693, forty-eight houses burned and four at Fittleton), Great Bedwyn (1716, about twenty-eight houses destroyed or badly damaged), Bradford-on-Avon (1742, several houses), Hindon (1754 'destroyed much of the town'), Heytesbury (*c.* 1769, sixty-five houses burned).

Storms were probably less important in causing rebuilding. In 1251 a roof louvre was blown down at Clarendon Palace. Buildings there were damaged by severe storms in the fourteenth century. Further storms in the county in the early seventeenth and early eighteenth centuries caused structural damage. Wars too, played their part. After 1139, raids between the castles of Devizes and Trowbridge in the war between the Empress Maud and Stephen of Blois were said to have reduced all the surrounding country to a 'lamentable desert'.

Sometimes houses are found to contain small fragments of an earlier building, such as a few timbers from framing or part of a cruck truss embedded in situ in an otherwise rebuilt wall. It has been suggested that this was to prove the continuity of the holding if there was a dispute about the rights or lands that went with it. At any period most houses are 'old', dating from earlier centuries, repaired and altered. So a survey of houses in the fifteenth century will mainly describe earlier buildings.

Restorations

It was probably not until the nineteenth century that efforts were made to return certain medieval houses to their original plan and appearance. This process continues today and now affects more minor buildings. This gives the visitor a wonderful feel of what it was like to walk into a medieval house. For the recorders of buildings though, restorations cause problems. Features may be moved around within the building or introduced from elsewhere. Examples are a hall fireplace now in the parlour at Bewley Court, and the front door to Sheldon Manor brought from a church in another county. Where the architects involved left a good record as they did in these instances, the task is simplified, but unrestored houses are often more informative and retain much of interest from succeeding centuries which is otherwise lost.

Building Materials

Stone

The limestone quarries – The west and north of Wiltshire are situated on the limestone belt running diagonally across England and the building stones found in this area were certainly exploited by the Romans, especially near Bath. In the Saxon and early medieval periods, stone quarrying does not seem to have been practised as a full-time continuous industry. Stone was not purchased as now from quarrymen, but rather land suitable for quarrying was bought or leased often from some distance away and worked when required for a particular building project. The material was jealously guarded by the Crown, and by the top levels of ecclesiastical and lay society. It is no accident that Box and Corsham were royal manors, the name Kingsdown at Box reflecting this. In this area lay the best ashlar limestone, ashlar being freestone with an even texture throughout which could be carved and worked in any direction and laid in precise regular blocks with little mortar.

The main quarry at Box was at Hazelbury and in the seventeenth century John Aubrey called it 'the eminentest free-stone quarrey in the West of England'. This is thought to have been the source of stone for the Saxon St Laurence's Church at Bradford-on-Avon, and it also supplied the stone used for Malmesbury Abbey, Stanley Abbey, Bradenstoke Priory, Lacock Abbey and Monkton Farleigh

Priory. The quarry was controlled by the Croke family at Hazelbury Manor by the mid-twelfth century and between about 1189 and 1306 they made various grants of quarries to religious houses. Grants were of varying sizes, for example a plot 23.1 m in length to line up with an existing quarry, or one or two acres. A Lacock Abbey grant was only for as long as the stone would last.

It is thought that there was an extension of the Box quarries in the mid-thirteenth century and the Bigot family, who also had quarry land, then made grants to Bradenstoke and Stanley. Royal use of the quarries continued. In 1254 the Sheriff of Wiltshire was ordered to carry six cartloads of Hazelbury stone to finish the king's works at Freemantle, Hampshire. In 1465, Thomas Tropenell acquired quarry land at Hazelbury before starting to build his manor house at Great Chalfield.

The Chilmark area was another source of freestone, supplying the south of the county. It provided stone for the Norman churches of the area, for Old Sarum Cathedral and for Salisbury Cathedral. Wilton Abbey already held the manor of Chilmark at the time of the Domesday Book and no doubt used the quarries for its own building. In 1358–9 the great hall at Clarendon Palace was repaired or rebuilt with Chilmark stone. Early fifteenth-century account rolls mention four or five quarries at Teffont Evias and some of the early stone of Chilmark type may be from there.

Quarrying was not restricted solely to the areas of the best freestone but it was always carefully controlled. In the early thirteenth century, William Earl Marshal (regent of Henry III) ordered

William de Brewer to allow the Abbot of Stanley to dig for stone in Earl William's wood of Cherhill and to have it conveyed for the building of the abbey church, but no injury was to be done to the forest. Early quarries can sometimes be recognized from their relationship with other features like roads and boundaries. Their distinctive characteristic is often a flat terrace on a hillside with a steep escarpment behind. Other quarries especially tile pits for roofing tiles, are depressions in the tops of hills. As the topsoil has been removed, most quarries have subsequently been left as wooded areas and the age of the trees can give an indication of when the quarry was abandoned. In the Avon valley from Bradford-on-Avon to Limpley Stoke, many old quarry areas can be detected, some very large. One of the biggest is at Avoncliff, and Cliff (or Cleeve) occurs in the names of the early quarry areas referring to the bare escarpment produced by quarrying. The earliest record of the name Avoncliff is from 1135 in the Shaftesbury Abbey records. Cleeve Rocks at Limpley Stoke are near one of the oldest tile quarries of the parish. Clyffe Pypard was called Clife as early as 983 and the manor was held by the Bishop of Winchester by 1086. There was Hodd's Clif at Chilmark in 860. A seventeenth-century map of Box has Gree Cliffe at Hazelbury and Wormscliffe, and two fields called Cleeves at Kingsdown. Seend Cleeve, so named from at least 1255, is the site of a sandstone quarry.

The use of stone — A characteristic of the early use of stone is that, being in short supply and expensive to transport, it was re-used over and over again. There is evidence nationally that in the eleventh and twelfth centuries, Roman stone was extensively re-used. At Salisbury, carved stone from the derelict castle and cathedral at Old Sarum was used first in the Close graveyard wall and then in the construction of the walls and gates of the Close in about 1327. Despite their high status, however, and a direction to build 'fair houses of stone', the builders of the canons' and other houses of the Close from 1213 onwards used dressed stone only sparingly, the bulk of the walls being generally of rubble of different kinds. The Abbot of Sherborne's house, now the Salisbury and South Wiltshire Museum, is special in having doorway and window surrounds made from the golden stone of Ham Hill in Somerset, a quarry area under the abbot's control (*no. 3*). The stone is more resistant to weathering than Wiltshire limestones.

In the medieval period, blocks of walling freestone were cut to a size that was easy to handle. This was commonly no more than 38 cm in each direction.

Stone tiles — Alec Clifton Taylor said that stone tiles or slates were used by the Romans, but not by the Saxons, and were rare in the thirteenth century and more common from the fourteenth century onwards. In 1296, Malmesbury Abbey's manor at Fowlswick had a kitchen and farm buildings 'covered in stone'. In 1311 the abbess of Lacock granted a vacant piece of ground in Lacock to an adjacent householder, 'whereon he shall raise and build at his own expense a competent house covered with stones'. In 1367, Shaftesbury Abbey bought five hundred stone tiles for tiling buildings at Barton Farm, Bradford-on-Avon, and in 1392, a further 2,100 tiles. For 1367 there is a reference to their remossing roofs. Some elaborate stone

No. 3 Fifteenth-century flint and stone banding and the remains of window surrounds in Ham Hill stone, 65 The Close, Salisbury.

No. 4 Chimney stack of about 1400 with stone and flint chequers at Castle Cottage, Great Bedwyn. Probably a remnant of St John the Baptist's Hospital. Note the older roof line on the side of the stack.

roof finials survive to the present day. The most spectacular ones, which depict knights and griffins, are at Great Chalfield Manor. Others, more eroded, are at Stowford Manor, Wingfield, and on medieval barns in the Bradford-on-Avon area.

Flint — Flint was extensively used for mass walling at Old Sarum and Salisbury. The King's House of the early twelfth century at Old Sarum had ashlar-faced flint rubble walls. The houses of the Close mainly have walls of whole flint nodules, intermixed with some brick tile and a small amount of limestone rubble, all set in large amounts of a mortar containing small pebbles. It is likely that such walls were plastered over or whitewashed when built, giving a uniform white appearance with only the freestone dressings visible. This was the case at Clarendon Palace where, by the thirteenth century, flint walls 1.2 m thick had been built. In the later Middle Ages, flintwork tended to be more regularly coursed with the flints more closely bedded together, and less mortar was used. Occasionally the flints were halved and set in chequers with alternating squares of dressed stone. This was a more expensive process and the walls would have been unplastered. Most local examples of this technique are post-medieval, but a few, including the chimney stack at Castle Cottage, Great Bedwyn (*no. 4*), are earlier. Another decorative technique was banding. The Abbot of Sherborne's house in the Close has some stone and flint banding on the facade, probably dating from the fifteenth century. Lowlier examples of the early use of flint at Littlecote have been cited (p. 18). Flint could be gathered on the surface without quarrying and was therefore used widely much earlier than other types of stone.

Chalk stone — In the post-medieval period the hardest chalk was much used for building, internally and wherever it was well protected. No medieval examples of its use as a main walling material have been noted locally, though it had been used in blocks and as rubble mixed with flints by the Romans. There are only examples of its use as a flooring material in medieval houses and as infilling to timber-framing at Salisbury.

Sarsen — Sarsen is a type of sandstone and is found in boulders scattered over some areas of the chalk downland of Wiltshire. Very little of it is now left in situ, but in the medieval period there must still have been a great deal. It is a very hard stone and no examples of its being shaped as a building stone during that period have been noted. Its main use was as a footing for timber-framed houses and especially for the main posts or crucks. The boulders were used largely as found.

Greensand — At Devizes the underlying greensand was hollowed out in the medieval period to form cellars. The hardest type there was also sometimes used in squared blocks for the plinths of medieval timber buildings. Ironstone, the hardest variety of all

which occurs at Seend and in Calne Without, was used for building in the post-medieval period. Though quarries were in existence, no early examples of its use in houses have been noted.

Cob — Cob is a mixture of mud and straw or mud and lime (derived from chalk), built up in layers and left to dry. It was used by the Romans in Wiltshire, for example in the outbuildings of Downton Roman villa in about AD 300. There is some archaeological evidence for its use in the medieval period but, since on decay it crumbles back to earth, it is not always easy to recognize. The daub of wattle-and-daub infill is a similar material with the addition of dung and cow hair.

Brick and tiles

Floor tiles — The earliest evidence of the medieval use of ceramic products in building in Wiltshire comes from a floor-tile kiln, constructed near Clarendon Palace in about 1237–1244. The kiln is now in the British Museum, with a segment of reconstructed chapel flooring and a pavement from the ground floor of the Queen's chamber block. From the thirteenth century, floor tiles were used extensively for the principal rooms of religious houses, and many Wiltshire examples of these very decorative encaustic tiles still exist. Typically they have heraldic devices on them or form geometric patterns when laid. They may also have been used for manor and town houses in the later Middle Ages.

Plain tiles — Salisbury City Council forbade the use of thatch in 1431 and 'tile' was used thereafter. These were probably plain tiles.

There is evidence for their use in London from the late twelfth century. The tiles were usually made at pottery kilns, and at Salisbury they could have come first from Laverstock where the kilns were in use from the twelfth to the fourteenth centuries. In the Close a number of houses have courses of tiles set herringbone fashion in the flint walls, or as a flat course to level up the wall below a window or at the eaves. The tiles were also used in the construction of kilns, for open hearths and in early fireplaces (see pp. 62–64). These uses confirm that they were being made locally by the early thirteenth century. At Marlborough, too, plain tiles were the main post-medieval roofing material, and the presence of early pottery kilns in the Savernake forest area suggests they could have been made and used earlier.

Ceramic ridge-tiles and finials — Where stone slates were used on medieval houses in the county, ceramic ridge tiles, usually glazed green, were often used as a decorative finish. It was probably cheaper to mould these inverted-V-shaped tiles from clay than to carve the shape from freestone. At Old Sarum, ridge-tiles glazed in shades of red and green were found. Other examples have been widely found in the county adjacent to good quality houses. They were normally crested, with knife slashes, and at the ends of the roof there were elaborate finials in the shape of people, animals, crosses or balls. A number of tile fragments of this kind were found when the kilns at Nash Hill, Lacock (WAM 69), and at Minety (WAM 68) and Laverstock were excavated. The Nash Hill kilns were probably set up for Lacock Abbey, but later supplied other monastic sites including Stanley Abbey. Evidence in other counties

suggests ceramic ridge-tiles were not made before the thirteenth century. In documents there are references to 'crests' and 'ridge tiles', but in some cases these would have been made from stone.

Bricks — Brick-making, though known to the Romans, was not re-introduced into Europe until the late twelfth century and appeared first in the east of England. The first-known building in the county made wholly of brick, however, appears to have been a lodge, now gone, built by Edward IV in the park around Clarendon Palace in 1465–7. No further examples in the county are known until the mid-sixteenth century.

Thatch

Thatch was by far the most common roofing material and seems to have been used in Southern England throughout the medieval period. A document mentions it at Winchester in 1161. A number of Wiltshire houses and cottages have been recorded with the original smoke-blackened thatch still surviving under later layers. Wheat straw was most often used, but reed has also been found, for example at Rose Cottage, Upavon. The latter might have been the cheaper material near a river or low-lying area. Medieval thatch in Wiltshire is in some cases attached to riven laths, and in others to sections of hurdling (*no. 5*). Laths, which used oak, were probably more expensive than hurdles.

Lead

Lead began to be regularly used as a roofing material for high-quality buildings in the last quarter of the twelfth century. It was

No. 5 The hall roof at Big Thatch, Ford, North Wraxall, showing original smoke-blackened thatch on hurdles.

being used for gutters, roof ridges and for sheeting roofs at Clarendon Palace by the 1230s, some having been mined in Derbyshire and transported via Southampton. In 1250, two ball finials of lead were put on the hall roof. Leadenhall, so-called presumably for its lead roof, was one of the earliest buildings of Salisbury Close.

Timber

Timber was the predominant building material of the Anglo-Saxon period and continued to be so over most of Wiltshire for the whole of the medieval period. The extent of forest land in the county has been described. Timber was in abundance, mostly oak and much of very good quality. The only areas of England that seem to have had even better timber are parts of the Midlands and the Weald.

Today, with timber scarce and mostly imported, it is always surprising to discover the quantity needed for a good-sized medieval house. In 1230 the king ordered Ralph, son of Nicholas, to have twenty-five oaks from the forest of Chippenham and the same from the forest of Melksham for his buildings at Corsham. There was a further grant of twenty oaks from these forests for his guest-house. The trunks would have been used for the main posts or crucks and the beams, with branches used for the lesser timbers. The religious houses conveyed building timber from one part of their estates to another. In 1376, timber for a new gatehouse with a chamber and palings for a new palisade were sent from Bradford-on-Avon to Shaftesbury.

Shingles and boards — Oak shingles were sometimes used as a roofing material. A new shingle roof was installed at Clarendon Palace in 1205–6, and between 1238 and 1252, 130,000 shingles were supplied from the forests of Downton, Gillingham (Dorset) and the New Forest. The shingles and thatch on the roofs of Marlborough Castle were replaced by stone in 1260. Margaret Wood cites references to weatherboarded roofs in the thirteenth century. Such a roof on a sixteenth-century industrial building has recently been found at West Lavington, so they may have been used in the county at an earlier date.

Timber to stone

It is clear from survivals that the best oak lasts to the present day as well as stone does, but timber buildings are always vulnerable in two places. The feet of the posts tend to rot, and the wattle and daub panels in the walls decay. For this reason there has always been a process in the life of a timber building whereby the walls from the bottom upwards are gradually replaced in stone or brick.

On the west side of Wiltshire, where there are good quarries, it is often assumed that there were stone houses of Cotswold appearance throughout the Middle Ages. This is, in general, not true. Buildings of the sixteenth century and earlier at Chippenham, Trowbridge, Lacock and Melksham were timber-framed. Before the sixteenth century many were timber-framed at Malmesbury, Calne, Colerne and in the Lyneham area (*no. 6*). In the towns and villages with the best quarries – Box, Corsham, Castle Combe, Bradford-on-Avon and Atworth – stone was quite widely used already in the fifteenth century, but there are sometimes remnants of even earlier timber buildings embedded in the walls. The same process took place near the quarries of south-west Wiltshire. Apshill House, Lower Chicksgrove, Tisbury, with a possibly late fourteenth century roof, was probably originally timber-framed.

Like most social processes, the use of quarried stone started with buildings of the highest status and ended with labourers' cottages. The castles at Ludgershall and Devizes were rebuilt in stone in the twelfth century. Manor houses near the stone quarries were rebuilt in the fourteenth century (some with royal or monastic connections

No. 6 *Timber mullioned window encased in the later stone wall at Trunnells Farm, Colerne. The mullions are chamfered and stopped.*

possibly in the thirteenth century). Sheldon Manor had a two-storey stone porch by about 1300. Bewley Court was largely converted to stone at the end of the fourteenth century (*no. 7*). Lesser manor houses a little farther from the quarries were converted in the fifteenth century, and yeoman's and tradesman's houses mainly in the sixteenth and seventeenth centuries.

Evidence for timber houses being converted to stone — A number of clues may point to the conversion of timber houses to stone, though the only firm evidence is when timbers survive in situ with mortices or pegholes for further vanished framing. Some

No. 7 Bewley Court, Lacock. The hall is to the left of the porch and the cross-wing with its first-floor Great Chamber to the right. The oriel window and battlements are a reconstruction, but the cylindrical chimney is original. (Plan, fig. 16.)

preceded the walls lies in mortices for wall posts under the ends of the tiebeams, but this is a position that can only rarely be examined.

It is obvious that difficulties and errors of interpretation can be caused when this process is not recognized. The roof of the original timber building may be dated too late by looking at the stone windows of the later walls. The room divisions indicated by the closed and open trusses of the roof may not conform to the rooms in existence below. Recording early stone houses is frequently more difficult than recording comparable timber ones. Where timber houses have been converted to brick, the process is often easier to recognize. The plinth will usually still be stone with brick above, again with vertical joints. Some timbers are more likely to be left visible as the walls will be thinner than stone walls.

pointers are: a thatched roof in an area with stone roofs; jagged vertical joints in the stonework where sections of wall were replaced between posts; a wider base to the wall which started out as the plinth of a timber wall (up to 1 m high), sometimes with a ledge left on the inside of the wall; a change in stonework part way up the wall; a roof type earlier than the doorway and window types; walling with original windows for two storeys, but the smoke-blackened roof of an open hall. Conclusive evidence that a roof

Types of Medieval Houses

Below is a list of some of the best surviving examples in the county. For a suggestion of those that can be visited, see later (p. 106).

Castles: Old Sarum, Ludgershall.

Manor houses and freehold estates: Bewley Court (early fourteenth century and *c*. 1390); Woodlands (fourteenth and fifteenth century); Sutton Veny; Bradfield; Great Chalfield; Norrington (*c*. 1377); Westwood; South Wraxall (fifteenth century and later); Parks Court, Upton Scudamore (*no. 8*); Sheldon; King John's House, Tollard Royal.

All these have stone outer walls and retain a generally medieval exterior appearance. Others with later walls, like Fowlswick Farm, Chippenham Without, are still excellent inside. A few retain timber outer walls, including Wick Cottage, Heddington, reduced from its original size (*no. 9*). At Barton Farm, Bradford-on-Avon; Brook Hall, Heywood, and Place Farm, Tisbury, the appearance of the main house has been more altered, but outbuildings and the courtyard arrangement still remain. The main hall at Brook has completely gone.

Bishop's palace: Salisbury (the *c*. 1220 undercroft remains). Canons' and church dignitaries' houses; Aula Le Stage; the North Canonry; the Old Deanery, Hemingsby; others in Salisbury Close.

No. 8 Parks Court, Upton Scudamore. The house of an ancient freehold estate held by the Park family from at least 1242. The base-cruck hall, probably of the early fourteenth century, is in the centre and has an oriel window.

No. 10 The Chantry, Mere, which housed three chantry priests. The service end and kitchen are to the right. The land for the building was acquired in 1424 and the house may be slightly later.

No. 9 Wick Cottage, Heddington, possibly the principal house of the small manor of Heddington Bohun. The house has a wing behind and formerly extended further to the left. The height of the wall in comparison to the roof suggests an early building which is confirmed by the two periods of cruck construction inside.

Monasteries: Lacock Abbey; the Priory at Kington St Michael; Bradenstoke Abbey.

Parsonages: Steeple Ashton; Bremhill; Yatton Keynell.

Chantries: 99 High Street, Marlborough; the Chantry, Mere (*no. 10*, land granted in 1424).

Gentry houses: Talboys, Keevil (*front cover*).

Town houses: Great Porch and 4 St John's Court, Devizes; many at Salisbury including 9 Queen Street (of *c.* 1306 and 1314, the oldest dateable house in the city), the Hall of John Hall (1470–83); 52–54 High Street. Black Barn and others at Steeple Ashton; various houses at Lacock and Castle Combe; 46 High Street, Cricklade; the Woodhouse, St Mary Street, Chippenham; 21–23 Church Street, Calne.

Shops: 63 Fore Street, Trowbridge and 7–8 The Shambles, Bradford-on-Avon (both refronted); 8 Queen Street, Salisbury (mid-fifteenth century, belonged to John Cammell, mayor 1449 and possibly grocer).

Inns: George and Dragon, Potterne; George Inn, New Inn and others at Salisbury; Sign of the Angel, Lacock (*no. 11*); Rose and Crown, Chippenham.

Farmhouses: Linfurlong, Rowde; 10 Coxhill Lane, Potterne (*no. 12*); Old Common Farm, Bromham; Big Thatch, Ford, North Wraxall.

Groups of cruck houses on adjoining plots: Church Street, Chiseldon; Canon Square, Melksham; High Street, Lacock.

Lodgings: Westwood Manor; Brook Hall, Heywood.

Gatehouses: Old Sarum (late twelfth century); Church Farm, Seagry; Archway Cottage, Castle Combe; Priory Barn, Bradford-on-Avon (only a pillar of the gate itself remains); Place Farm, Tisbury.

Porch House, Potterne and King John's Hunting Lodge at Lacock are well-preserved, high-status houses, but their history is not sufficiently known to put them in a category.

No. 11 The Sign of the Angel at Lacock, a fifteenth-century inn of courtyard plan. The left gable is earlier and jettied. In the background is 3 Church Street, a house of cruck construction.

No. 12 10 Coxhill Lane, Potterne, of about 1500. The curved timbers of a cruck truss are visible in the gable wall. The dormer window with close studding was added in about 1600 and the left end of the house was altered in the nineteenth century. (Plan, fig. 6.)

Plans

Aisled plans

Aisled plans existed in the Anglo-Saxon period but were possibly re-introduced by royalty in the late eleventh century, spreading across from the east of England where they remained more widely used. The halls at the Bishop's Palace, Old Sarum (1102–39), Clarendon Palace (1181–3), Devizes Castle (first mentioned 1236–7, *fig. 4*) and Ludgershall Castle (1244) were aisled. At Old Sarum the hall was 27.4 m long, the 'nave' 6.4 m wide and the aisles 3.7 m. The piers were probably rectangular with twisted shafts at the angles, the arches had moulded orders and ornamental hood mouldings, and the aisles were probably vaulted. The hall must have very much resembled a church. At Clarendon the hall was 25 m long with a width, including the aisles, of 15.8 m.

The only known partially surviving, fully aisled house in Wiltshire is Old House, the former manor house of Edington Priory's estate at Market Lavington. The hall is 10.7 m long by 6.9 m wide, and has a spere truss, with short partitions protecting the hall from draughts. It has been dated to the early fourteenth century. The Old Courthouse at Castle Combe appears to have had a single aisle at the rear. A possible early fourteenth-century document in the Edington Cartulary mentions a house at Edington, 18.3 m long and 12.2 m wide, which therefore could also have been aisled. No doubt there were many more aisled houses, but it is a difficult plan to modernize into a two-storey building. The aisles were always likely to be

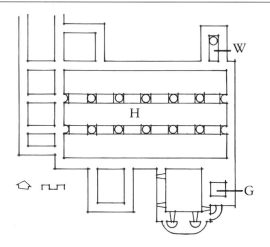

*Fig. 4 The aisled hall of Devizes Castle at scale 1:500, based on a plan in '**Devizes Castle**' by E.H. Stone, 1920. The plan was recovered through excavation and the doorway positions are not known. The room next to the garderobe was a plastered apartment.*

removed and would have left little trace, especially if the walls were rebuilt in stone. The tendency to build with aisles continued in barns in the non-limestone area of Wiltshire until the nineteenth century.

Further west than Wiltshire the only aisled houses known are the early twelfth century part of the royal palace at Cheddar in Somerset, a hall (after 1200), two stone halls, one in Baldwin Street and the single-aisled Colston's House at Bristol, and the Bishop's Palaces at Exeter (c. 1224–44) and at Wells (1274–92).

Halls with chambers

Whether aisled or not, early halls usually had chambers at one or both ends. About 1257, an IPM records at Market Lavington: 'A certain long house in the place of a hall, and one room in one head, and another room in another head, and one outer room and one cowhouse'. It was said then to be old and in a bad state. At Berwick (St James?) in the same year, there was 'one hall, 2 rooms at one head of the hall near the land, and one room on the upper floor and a cellar underneath in another head'. Fowlswick Manor was rebuilt between 1268 and 1296 with 'a hall, and a central

No. 13 Fowlswick Farm (formerly Manor), Chippenham Without. The hall range to the left, of base-cruck construction, was encased in stone in the sixteenth century and the dormers and doorway were added in 1679. The cross-wing next right may have been altered to stone in the fifteenth century. The second cross-wing was added before 1630.

chamber between two chambers at the gable of that hall'. An altered crosswing is there still (*no. 13*). Old House, Market Lavington, has a contemporary two-storey cross-wing. At Norridge, Upton Scudamore, in 1333, the manor house consisted of a hall with various chambers, a chapel, a kitchen and a dovehouse.

Sometimes in the eleventh to thirteenth centuries there was a separate detached chamber or 'camera' near the hall having one or two storeys. The tall, unheated building at Garsdon Manor, Lea and Cleverton, with base cruck and crown-post roof, and attached by its corner to the main house, may have been such a building. The manor was a grange of Malmesbury Abbey and a 'camera' would have been suitable accommodation for the abbot during visits, or for his steward.

First-floor halls

A first-floor hall was a Norman plan suitable for castles and other defensive houses, but which came to be used even for manor houses and town houses. At 86 Lower Westwood, Westwood, a cellar or undercroft under a later house has two arches separated by a circular pillar (*fig. 5*). The pillar appears to be in situ and to date from the late twelfth century. Above the room there is likely to have been a first-floor hall of stone or timber. Westwood was a manor of Winchester Abbey, and Henry of Blois, brother of King Stephen, was Bishop of Winchester between 1129–71 and known for his building in stone. At Alvediston in about 1200 there was a house called 'Staenhihalle'. This indicates a tall stone house,

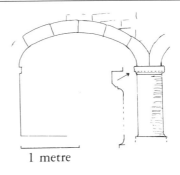

Fig. 5 *Section of the central Romanesque circular pillar and one of the adjoining arches in the cellar at 86 Lower Westwood, Westwood.*

1 metre

possibly a first-floor hall. King John's House at Tollard Royal had a first-floor hall and is thought to date from about 1240.

Longhouses and three-room and cross-passage plans

A longhouse, as understood today, is a dwelling divided by a cross-passage into a living section and a cattle house. The animals entered through the same doorway as the people, so the passage is wide. The living section may be a single room, but more often comprises a hall and an inner chamber. Longhouses have been excavated in the county (see p. 18), but no definite surviving examples are known. There are farmhouses with attached eighteenth-century barns, and at Daubeneys, Colerne, the medieval house has a cruck-built stable attached, but the cross-passage is within the house and not shared. It seems likely that longhouses in Wiltshire largely ceased to be used or built after the thirteenth century, though a few may have

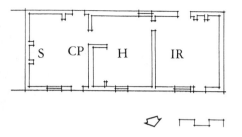

Fig. 6 Plan of 10 Coxhill Lane, Potterne, a cruck cottage. The service end was originally twice as long. All fireplaces are post-medieval.

remained. In 1612, Pound Farm at Stanley, Bremhill, was described as a house and oxhouse of five bays, four of them lofted. In the north and west of the British Isles some longhouses in remote areas have remained in use until the present day.

The three-room and cross-passage plan is similar but has a services end in place of the byre. This plan was very common for yeomen's farmhouses in the fourteenth and fifteenth centuries, petering out at the end of the sixteenth century. Where space allowed, it was also used in towns. Examples are 10 Coxhill Lane, Potterne (*fig. 6*); Orchard Farm, West Overton; Big Thatch, Ford; and Linfurlong, Rowde. These mostly have long service ends. A relic of the longhouse was the use of the terms 'high end' and 'low end' in such houses. From the cross-passage there was a step up into the hall so

that the byre could not drain in that direction. In the hall there was sometimes a dais at the far end where the head of the household and his family ate their meals. There might be a further step up to the inner room or parlour. The service end normally became a kitchen in the sixteenth or seventeenth century. In a three-room and cross-passage plan, therefore, the evidence to look for to see if the building was a longhouse includes a drain in the end-wall of the services end, a wide cross-passage, and the building of a kitchen behind the house instead of converting the services, or the use of the inner room as a kitchen.

Two-room plans

The farmhouses of husbandmen in Wiltshire, the lesser farmers who were sometimes also tradesmen, usually had only two rooms, though sometimes with a workshop attached. These rooms were the heated hall, and an unheated parlour or inner room used for sleeping and storage. The plan is frequent among fifteenth-century, rural, timber-framed houses, for example 88–90 Chilton Foliat; the Green Dragon, Fittleton; and The Cottage, Fovant. There are likely also to have been very lowly, one-room houses like the labourer's dwellings of the seventeenth century and later, but no evidence for them has been found.

Hall and cross-wing plans

Hall and cross-wing plans had earlier origins (as in the late thirteenth century at Fowlswick), but had become widely popular by the fifteenth century in Wiltshire. Sometimes they were alterations of earlier houses with three rooms in line. A cramped parlour was demolished and rebuilt as a cross-wing, having a parlour with a service room behind on the ground floor, and a great chamber at the front with a small chamber behind on the first floor. In the fifteenth century, Great Porch, Devizes (*no. 14 and fig. 7*); Talboys, Keevil (*front cover and fig. 8a*); and 9–10 Church Street, Trowbridge were built with this plan. Sheldon Manor was converted to such a plan, the front part of the new wing blocking a lancet window of the porch (*fig. 8b*). The plan remained popular in the sixteenth century.

No. 14 Great Porch, Devizes, a jettied hall and cross-wing house of the early fifteenth century with parts of the facade later replaced in brick. The timberwork is all of high quality. The cross-wing has a scissor-braced panel and formerly had a projecting first-floor window. (Plan, fig. 7.)

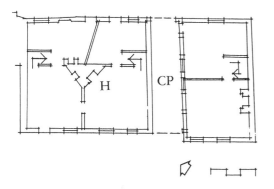

Fig. 7 Plan of Great Porch, Devizes, based on a drawing by Richard Warmington. The hall was later divided into four rooms as shown. Below the cross-wing is an original cellar.

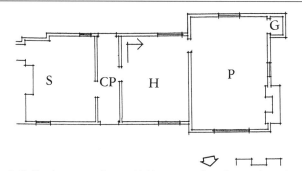

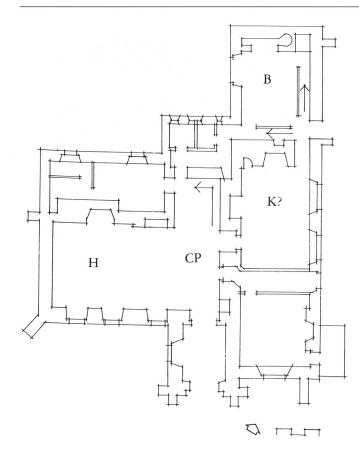

Fig. 8 Hall and cross-wing plans (*a*) Sheldon Manor, Chippenham Without. The rooms to the rear of the hall and cross-passage are later, (*b*) Talboys, Keevil.

Wealden houses

Wiltshire is on the fringe of the south-east England area of compact, Wealden-type houses, built between the early fourteenth century and about 1520. These had a cross-wing at each end and an open hall between, with characteristic bracing across the recessed portion of the front. Wiltshire examples are thought to date from the late fifteenth or early sixteenth centuries and are limited to three, all in towns: 25 North Street (*no. 15*) and 19 South Street, Wilton; 66 St Ann's Street, Salisbury. Porch House, Potterne, is not a Wealden house, but has some similarities of plan (*no. 16 and fig. 9*).

No. 16 Porch house, Potterne, of the late fifteenth century, drawn by Owen Carter in 1850. The cross-wings and porch are jettied and the facade is close studded. (Plan fig. 9.)

No. 15 Old postcard of 25 North Street, Wilton, a small house of Wealden plan. A gallery at the rear of the central hall links the wings.

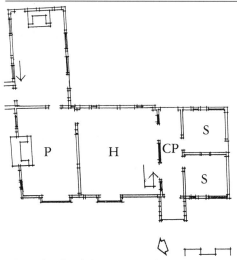

Fig. 9 Plan of Porch House, Potterne. The rear wing is later.

Town plans

On confined burgage plots and other town sites, houses often had to be built end on to the street. There was sometimes a shop at the front with a chamber above it, the hall behind and further rooms to the rear. A fifteenth-century example is 6–7 Kingsbury Street, Marlborough. A variation on a wider plot was to have two matching houses with shops at the front, as at 63 Fore Street, Trowbridge, and 8 Queen Street, Salisbury (*no. 17*). Another example, but one that has been refronted, is 7–8 The Shambles, Bradford-on-Avon. A post-medieval alteration often seen involves the fronts of two adjoining medieval houses having been rebuilt as a larger new house and the older rear portions having been retained as wings. An older wing with crucks survives at Unicorn House, Malmesbury. At Salisbury there was sometimes a house at the front of the plot, a courtyard behind and a further hall at the rear of the yard. Inns also had courtyards, usually with galleried lodgings along the side. The George Inn at Trowbridge was originally like this.

Another town plan that continued after the medieval period was for the house to have a central entrance, with a hall on one side of the passage and a parlour on the other. An example is 46 High Street, Cricklade (*c.* 1500), and 6–8 Monday Market Street, Devizes (now gone), is said to have been similar. The plan is a town version of the rural gentry house plan found extensively in Somerset and occasionally in Wiltshire, for example at Easton Court Farm, Corsham, and probably at Manor Farm, Yatton Keynell. At the latter there was a hall on one side of the passage and a solar over

No. 17 8 and 9 Queen Street, Salisbury. No. 8, to the right and jettied on first and second floors, may have been acquired by John Cammell, a grocer, in 1397. No 9 was built soon after 1306 by William Russel and he raised its height around 1314. It has a simple hammer-beam roof.

services on the other. Where plots allowed, town houses had plans parallel to the street similar to those of rural houses. Great Porch and 39 New Park Street at Devizes, and 8 Church Street, Lacock, are some examples.

Other elements of the plan

The manor houses and gentry houses often had a number of other rooms of varying sizes apart from the hall, services, parlour and great chamber or solar. As an alternative, some of the functions could be carried out in separate buildings on the site.

Oriels — Oriels were small rooms off the upper end of the hall where the family dined. A good example survives at Bewley Court, Lacock. John Aubrey in 1670 said that they were in all the old Gothic halls of north Wiltshire and mentioned Draycot (Cerne), Lackham (*fig. 10*) and Alderton. 'Oriel' windows were a type of projecting window much used for oriels but also for other rooms.

Towers — Towers and tower houses were less often built in Wiltshire than in some other areas of England. There are two examples which have now gone. One was at the Manor House, Stanton St Quintin (*fig. 11*), where the tower was attached to the main building and may have been a camera as it seems to have housed a chamber over a strong room. The other was in the Old

45

Stourton House courtyard complex as drawn by John Aubrey. Such towers were fashionable but were probably also useful for security and to watch hunting.

Fig. 10 Old Lackham House, Lacock, in 1790, a drawing by Edward Kite after Grimm, in Wiltshire Notes and Queries, Vol. 3, 1899. The hall is to the left of the porch and was shown crenellated in a drawing of 1684.

Fig. 11 Old Manor House, Stanton St Quintin, from Aubrey and Jackson's Wiltshire Collection of 1862, redrawn by E. Kite from John Aubrey's seventeenth-century original.

Garderobes — Garderobes were sometimes store-rooms in the sense of the modern wardrobe. At Bewley Court in 1418 there was a very long list of military equipment, drapery, clothing and other lumber in the garderobe. The term is also used for latrines and these were common in houses of high status. First-floor examples without fittings survive at Black Barn, Steeple Ashton; Talboys, Keevil (*no. 18*); Lower Berrycourt Farm, Donhead St Mary, and elsewhere. More often there was a latrine pit in the garden, the forerunner of the privy. At Old Sarum, many layers of quick-lime were excavated from a latrine. A latrine was excavated at Raddon, Fyfield. It was an oval pit, 1.5 m by 1.2 m and 0.5 m deep, partly surrounded by the fairly large stake holes of a wooden structure. The rather 'rich' filling included a prick spur. Documents show that in 1395 the rector and convent of Edington were required to demolish the main latrine of the vicarage house at Keevil and reconstruct it in a place more convenient for the vicar's use.

No. 18 Garderobe tower on the side of the cross-wing at Talboys, Keevil.

Chapels — Many manor houses were next to the parish church or, like Southwick Court in the thirteenth century, had a private chapel in the garden. Others had an oratory or chapel within the house for which they had to obtain a licence from the bishop. Houses where oratories are known or suggested include Stowford Manor, Wingfield (first floor); Porch House, Potterne (over the porch); and the Rogers' manor house at Bradford-on-Avon (first floor). At Bewley Court there was a chamber over the chapel but at Woodlands, Mere, the detached chapel has a chamber below it and documents show that Keevil Manor had a similar arrangement in 1397. This was sometimes but not always for the priest. It is often thought that parts of old houses were chapels merely because they retain medieval windows. This has been suggested of the north wing of Barton Farm, Bradford-on-Avon, but there is no other evidence and the upper room is more likely to have been a great chamber.

Kitchens — Kitchens, too, were frequently detached buildings, sometimes linked to the house by a pentice (a single-pitched roof built against the house) or roofed passage. At Great Porch, Devizes, a post behind the hall appears to be the start of such a passage and there is no place for a kitchen within the house. Later in the history of a house a detached kitchen often became a brewhouse or the area between it and the house was infilled to create a further room. Keevil Manor in 1397 had a detached Great Kitchen 'newly repaired'. At the Chantry, Mere, the kitchen is unusually situated as a cross-wing beyond the service end of the house.

Lodgings — Maurice Barley has suggested that lodging ranges were a fourteenth and fifteenth-century development. The best example remaining in Wiltshire is at Brook Hall, Heywood (*no. 19*), dating from the late fifteenth century. It had stabling on the ground floor, and separate chambers with garderobes behind on the first floor. Only the principal chamber has a fireplace. The long building called Knights Chamber at Keevil Manor in 1397 has already been mentioned.

Gatehouses — Where a manor house had a courtyard or series of courtyards, and possibly also a moat, there was scope for an impressive gatehouse. This sometimes contained accommodation for a porter. At the Rogers' Manor, Bradford-on-Avon, the Priory Barn stands against the former gateway and retains a gate pillar. The building has a house at the gate end and possibly a wool loft or warehouse at the other. A similar gateway with adjoining building (now the main house) is at Kings Old Rectory, Broad Chalke. Bradfield Manor, Hullavington had a gatehouse depicted by John Aubrey. South Wraxall Manor has a fine gatehouse (*fig. 12*) and so has Place Farm, Tisbury (*no. 20*). At Tisbury there is also a smaller inner gatehouse. Archway Cottage is a gatehouse to the castle at Castle Combe (*no. 21*) and another for the rectory there is pictured in Scrope's history of the town (*fig. 13*). A gatehouse at Church Farm, Lower Seagry, Seagry, which belonged to Bradenstoke Abbey, is now a farm building.

Other outbuildings — Manor houses also often had stabling, dovecotes, barns and other farmbuildings, and sometimes dairies, malthouses, bakehouses and brewhouses.

No. 19 *Late fifteenth-century lodging range at Brook Hall, Heywood, where retainers or visiting guests were accommodated.*

No. 20 *Outer gatehouse at Place Farm, Tisbury, a grange of the abbess of Shaftesbury. There is a wagon entrance and a smaller pedestrian gateway.*

Fig. 12 *Gatehouse, South Wraxhall Manor, from Elyard, Some Old Wiltshire Homes, 1894*

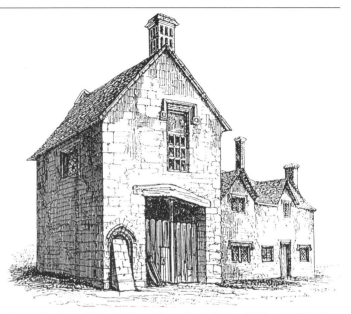

No. 21 Gateway Cottage, Castle Combe, one of the entrances to the castle. The gateway is of timber-framed, possibly base-cruck, construction.

Fig. 13 Gatehouse adjoining the Rectory House, Castle Combe pulled down in 1836. From Scrope's History of Castle Combe, 1852. A spiral stone stair led to the first floor and some timber-framing remained at the rear of the building.

Features

Walls

Timber — Most timber-framed houses have the walls in rectangular panels. In the medieval period the panels were often very large compared with sixteenth or seventeenth-century work. For example at 63 Fore Street, Trowbridge, 1.3 m by 1.1 m has been recorded, and at The Thatch, Ogbourne Maisey in Ogbourne St Andrew parish, panels are about 1.1 m wide by 1.1 m tall. Within the panels there are usually braces to support the main posts (*fig. 14*). Fourteenth-century parallel bracing occurs at 52 High Street, Salisbury (*no. 22*). St Andrew's Cross or scissor bracing is found at Salisbury; at Great Porch, Devizes (*no. 14*) and at Porch House, Lacock. The most common types of bracing, however, are arch bracing and tension bracing, arch bracing in general being the earlier, in use probably from the late thirteenth century onwards. A good example of tension bracing is in the end wall of Black Barn Farm, Steeple Ashton (*no. 23*).

No. 22 52–54 High Street, Salisbury, a fourteenth-century corner tenement with tension-bracing and parallel-bracing. In 1341 there were 'shops adjoining' and it was leased by a spicer to Walter de Upton.

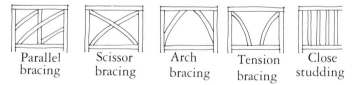

Parallel bracing   Scissor bracing   Arch bracing   Tension bracing   Close studding

Fig. 14 Bracing patterns in timber-framing, and close studding.

No. 23 Side view of Black Barn (Farm), Steeple Ashton, showing framing with tension braces, collar and tie-beam roof truss and rear wing with buttressed stone ground floor. There is a probable garderobe tower in the angle next to the wing.

The infill of the panels was usually wattle and daub, with upright staves set in a groove in the bottom timber of the panel and sprung into holes in the underside of the rail above. Wattles were then woven across. All wattle and daub in a house may not be original. For example it was sometimes added into open trusses when halls were partitioned into smaller rooms. The knowledge of how to make it seems to have lasted until the late eighteenth and even nineteenth centuries in the county, though it ceased to be used for new partitioning in good houses by the sixteenth or seventeenth centuries. At Salisbury, examples of chalk rubble infill have been found, for example at 52–54 High Street and 9 Queen Street, both fourteenth-century buildings. The rubble was held in place by long pegs.

In medieval rural buildings the walls were often only two panels high when the building had a single storey open to the roof. In later centuries three and then four panels high were used. As an alternative to panels, close studding was sometimes used. The vertical studs may be widely spaced in the cheapest form, as at a cottage at Hodson, Chiseldon, or set very close together as they are at Porch House, Potterne. One of the earliest examples known in the county was the former west wall of Bewley Court, Lacock, probably dating from the first half of the fourteenth century. This had room for a brace between the corner post and the first stud. The wall was photographed and drawn by Harold Brakspéar before removal (WAM 37). A series of pegs along a wallplate may indicate former close studding when the wall has been rebuilt in stone. This is the case at the Old Manor, West Lavington.

The thickened jowls at the tops of the posts of medieval houses are a subject worthy of more study. At 63 Fore Street, Trowbridge, they are very heavy, but at The Thatch, Ogbourne Maisey, they have a very gradual slope. Joints, too, need more study. In the Close at Salisbury, examples of the early, 'trait de Jupiter' scarf joints can be seen. At 63 Fore Street, Trowbridge, the scarf joints are edge-halved with under-squinted abutments.

Many town houses and a few rural houses were jettied, that is the upper floor projected over the lower floor. Jettying is thought to have still been a novelty in the early fourteenth century. Examples of that date occur in the vanished west wall of the solar at Bewley Court and at the George Inn, Salisbury. At 52 High Street, Salisbury, a fourteenth-century corner site, two adjoining walls are jettied. In the fifteenth century, many more examples occurred: Great Porch, Devizes; Porch House, Potterne (*no. 24*); Talboys, Keevil; the Woodhouse, Chippenham; Old Common Farm, Bromham; and The Sanctuary and many other houses at Steeple Ashton can be cited among others. Old drawings depict jettied houses at Calne and Malmesbury. In most of Wiltshire there was little jettying of floors above the ground-floor/first-floor level. This is more common in other parts of England, but there are examples at Salisbury (for example 8 Queen Street) where narrow town plots made the practice more useful. Jettying continued in the sixteenth and until the mid-seventeenth centuries.

In the fifteenth century and later, carved bargeboards were used to protect the ends of the purlins protruding through a gable roof truss (*no. 25*).

No. 24 Jetty construction with moulded bressummer at Porch House, Potterne.

When timber frames were prepared and assembled, carpenters marks were used to indicate the positions of the timbers. These were placed on the fair face of the timbers (the side where the pegs were driven in). On most timbers the marks can be seen with a little experience of knowing where to look. They are usually Roman numerals. On the earliest houses, long incised lines crossing from one timber to its matching twin can usually be seen. Sometimes there are straight lines on one timber and straight lines with half circles attached on the adjoining one. Another type has straight lines on one timber and lines with short lines attached at an angle on the other (*no. 26*). At the Old Vicarage, Bremhill, the marks are unusual, resembling a rounded M, with the largest

No. 25 Carved bargeboards at Porch House, Potterne, drawn by Owen Carter in 1850.

12.5 cm tall (*no. 27*). Sometimes in the fifteenth century, circles were used in conjunction with lines. At 46 High Street, Cricklade, arabic numbering was used.

Stone — Thickness is often a useful guide to the age of stone walls in Wiltshire, in the medieval period as much as later. Norman castle walls could be up to 3.7 m thick as they are at Old Sarum. In the fifteenth century the stone walls of houses were usually about 0.9 m thick. They often had a batter on the inside of the wall so that it sloped back becoming thinner higher up. The stone plinths of timber-framed buildings were often treated in this way, for example in the cross-wing at the Sanctuary, Steeple Ashton.

Medieval stonework was often faced with good ashlar and repairs can be detected by the use of rubble stone. This is the case on the south front of Bewley Court. At Steeple Ashton, the plinths of the timber-framed buildings are of unusually good stone and often buttressed (*no. 23*). Buttresses are normally found only at the roof truss positions and gable ends of stone houses. They were especially useful where the roofs were stone tiled or where there were open trusses inside and there was a lot of outward thrust. Where windows and doorways have been modernized, a buttress may be the first clue to the existence of a medieval house.

Some medieval houses had crenellations at the level of the eaves, giving a castle-like appearance. Because this could be seen as a form of fortification, a royal licence was required. At South Wraxall Manor there is a plain parapet with a series of grotesque gargoyles to drain the area behind it.

No. 26 Carpenter's marks on the wall-framing of the side-wall of 12 Bridewell Street, Devizes.

No. 27 Incised carpenter's marks resembling Ms on the main crown-post at the Old Vicarage, Bremhill, possibly of the early fourteenth century. Later whitewash makes the marks stand out.

Mortar and external plaster — Mortars varied considerably in their composition and require more study. A very hard external plaster with a swirled texture, called 'wormhole' or 'vermiculated' plaster, was sometimes applied to walls of flint or poor-quality stone.

Porches

Porches were a feature of high status lay and ecclesiastical houses and are thought to have become fashionable from the late twelfth and thirteenth centuries. The oldest domestic porch in the county is usually considered to be the two-storey stone porch at Sheldon Manor, Chippenham Without (*no. 28*). The ground-floor ceiling is a fairly plain stone vault with ribs resting on shafts with capitals

No. 28 Porch of about 1300 at Sheldon Manor, Chippenham Without. The box sundial on the gable dates from the eighteenth century.

(*no. 29*). It formerly had an outside stair to the upper room which suggests this was the room of the priest of the detached chapel some yards away.

An early fourteenth century, two-storey stone porch survives at Hemingsby, 56 The Close, Salisbury. The porch at Norrington Manor of about 1377 has a stone vault more elaborate than that at Sheldon, and so does the Abbot of Sherborne's house, 65 The Close, Salisbury (*c.* 1475–1504) which has fan vaulting with grotesque animal carvings. There was formerly a two-storey stone porch at Bradfield Manor, Hullavington, drawn by John Aubrey, and one with a battlemented oriel window to the first floor at Old Lackham House (*fig. 10*). Two-storey porches survive at Bewley Court (*no. 30*), South Wraxall Manor and Woodlands Manor, Mere. The single-storey early fifteenth-century stone porch to the prioress's house survives at Kington St Mary Priory. At Stowford Manor, Wingfield, the remains of a pillared entrance may have formed a shallow porch.

One of the earliest timber-framed porches may be the jettied example at Porch House, Lacock, possibly of the early fifteenth century. It has massive curved timbers forming the door arch and cross bracing above (*no. 31*). Great Porch, Devizes, has the mortices for the attachment of a porch at the front and carved paterae (flowers) which would have been visible inside the porch over the entrance door, but the porch was removed and the doorway and internal passage converted to an open passageway when a court of houses was built in the garden behind. Porch House at Potterne retains its fifteenth-century two-storey timber porch. Another at Manor Farmhouse, Berwick Bassett, has tension braces.

No. 29 *Interior of the porch at Sheldon Manor.*

No. 30 *Porch of about 1399, with the doorway in a square, castellated surround at Bewley Court, Lacock.*

No. 31 Timber-framed porch with scissor-braced panels and curved cruck-like timbers forming the entrance at Porch House, Lacock.

No. 32 Internal doorway, thought to be thirteenth century, at King John's Hunting Lodge, 21 Church Street, Lacock.

No. 33 Shouldered doorway, possibly fifteenth century, and adjoining cruck blade set on or in the ground at Wick Cottage, Heddington.

Doorways

Most of the earliest doorways have two-centred 'pointed' arched heads. The thirteenth-century doorway at King John's Hunting Lodge, 21 Church Street, Lacock (no. 32), is a remarkable survival with massive timbers. It was one of a pair and there is evidence for a similar pair above on the first floor. These doorways probably led from a screens passage and gallery above into a cross-wing or end section of the house. At Wick Cottage, Heddington, another unusual timber doorway has a kind of shouldered arch (no. 33). More conventional stone shouldered arches of a type found in the fifteenth century and around 1500 were at the Rogers' Manor,

No. 36 *Stone doorway with square, shafted surround of about 1399 from the staircase into the porch chamber at Bewley Court, Lacock.*

No. 35 *Stone doorway of about 1399 from the cross-passage into the cross-wing at Bewley Court, Lacock. The Great Chamber is jettied out over the cross-passage on stone coving.*

No. 34 *Round-arched doorway, probably early fourteenth century, with moulding and broach stops, leading on to the gallery at Bewley Court, Lacock.*

Bradford-on-Avon, in the house and 'barn'. At Bewley Court, Lacock, a timber round-arched doorway seems to be a relic of two surviving at the beginning of the twentieth century from the early fourteenth-century house (*no. 34*). It has elongated broach stops at the feet of the jambs on the best side. From the 1390s rebuilding of the house in stone there are a number of doorways, some with pointed heads and some with four-centred Tudor arches (*nos. 35 and 36*). This was a period of transition.

Occasionally doorways, especially exterior ones, were decorated with carved heads. A good example is at 8 Church Street, Lacock (*no. 37*), possibly of the fourteenth century. A doorway of 1431

59

No. 37 *Entrance doorway with carved heads at the ends of the hood moulding at 8 Church Street, Lacock. The house dates from the fourteenth century and the lack of first-floor windows indicates that it was a single-storey building with an open hall.*

No. 38 *Doorway with nicked head of 1431 into the first floor of the cross-wing at Sheldon Manor, Chippenham Without.*

No. 39 *Late fifteenth-century chamfered doorway into the possible warehouse or wool loft in the gatehouse range of the Rogers' manor at the 'Priory Barn', Bradford-on-Avon.*

with a chamfered surround at Sheldon Manor has a nicked head (*no. 38*). At the end of the fifteenth century, doorways with wider chamfered surrounds or wide hollow moulded surrounds began to appear and continued to be popular in the early sixteenth century. Examples can be seen at Iford Manor, Westwood; Hill House Farm, Box; and the Priory barn, Bradford-on-Avon (*no. 39*).

Windows

Some of the best-preserved early timber windows have been discovered buried in the middle of stone walls. They were originally part of a timber building later encased in stone (*nos. 6 and 40*). Many medieval windows had tall narrow lights, often trefoil-headed (*nos. 41 and 42*). Simple lancet windows of one to four lights carved out of one piece of stone have been recorded in the county in post-medieval positions, usually in outbuildings; *No. 72* in *Wiltshire Farm Buildings 1500–1900* is an example. Some may have been re-used from houses. Such windows are thought to have been made from the late twelfth to at least the sixteenth centuries, with fourteenth and fifteenth-century examples sometimes having sunken spandrels.

In the fifteenth century, cinquefoil heads to windows became common (*no. 43*) and occasionally there were small quatrefoil windows lighting stairs or providing a look-out (*no. 44*). Windows lighting the hall or a solar were usually larger than those in other positions. One way of increasing the light was to have an arched surround with a top light of quatrefoil or other design (*no. 45*). Some large halls, like Bradfield, Hullavington, had two or three

No. 40 Timber window with four trefoil-headed lights, possibly late thirteenth or fourteenth century, which had been encased in a later stone wall at Sparrows Barton, Easton, Corsham.

No. 41 Two-light trefoil-headed first-floor window at 46 High Street, Cricklade. The points of the cusps have been lost.

No. 42 Side window to the porch, Sheldon Manor, Chippenham Without.

No. 43 *Late fifteenth-century cinquefoil-headed window to the gatehouse at the 'Priory Barn', Bradford-on-Avon.*

No. 44 *Small quatrefoil window at the Priory, Kington St Michael.*

No. 47 *Late fifteenth-century windows in the remaining wall of the Rogers' manor house, Market Street, Bradford-on-Avon.*

No. 45 *First-floor window at the Chantry, 35 Church Street, Westbury, rectory manor house of the chanter of Salisbury Cathedral. It has a hood mould and vertical bars between the tracery, similar to a window of about 1377 at Norrington Manor, Alvediston.*

No. 46 *Oriel window of the hall, Porch House, Potterne.*

arched windows. There are smaller versions in the gatehouse at Place Farm, Tisbury (*no. 20*).

An alternative to arched heads was to have a two-tier mullioned and transomed design with four similar lights. The two-tier bay window at Porch House, Potterne, has extremely intricate decoration and would have provided a light and pleasant atmosphere for those dining inside (*no. 46*). The older form of projecting oriel window of canted or semi-circular plan is best seen at Great Chalfield Manor, Atworth, though the date is similar to that of Porch House (*also see frontispiece*). A cinquefoil-headed oriel window exists at Parks Court, Upton Scudamore, (*no. 8*). At the end of the fifteenth century, round-headed mullioned windows were introduced. These occur at Brook Hall (*no. 19*) and at The Priory, Bradford-on-Avon (*no. 47*).

Within the house there were sometimes windows giving borrowed light to the stairways or other dark areas. At The Chantry, 99 High Street, Marlborough, an internal two-light wooden window with cinquefoil heads lights the stair. At Great Chalfield Manor; Porch House, Potterne; Barton Farm, Bradford-on-Avon; and the Old Vicarage, Steeple Ashton, there were spy windows from the private quarters onto the hall.

Glass was a luxury in the Middle Ages. It is known to have been used in the thirteenth century. There was a contract for the making of a glass window for Marlborough Castle in 1237. Most medieval windows had only shutters, though horn or parchment were sometimes used. By the fifteenth century the better manor houses seem to have had some heraldic glass, particularly in the halls. An

No. 48 Unblocked window of about 1500 with some original diamond-leaded lights with green glass. Hill House Farm, Box.

unblocked window to the solar at Hill House Farm, Box (*no. 48*), still has its original green glass.

Open fires

When a house had an open hall, the fire was made on a prepared hearth in the middle of the room or against a stone in the middle of one end-wall of the room. Sometimes such hearths have been found during excavations or renovation work. In the twelfth-century aisled hall of the King's House at Old Sarum, the hearth was in the second bay from the North. The dais from which the fire was enjoyed was 2.4 m wide and 0.6 m above floor level. At the Old

Deanery, Salisbury (thirteenth century and later), there were three superimposed hearths in a central position near the dais end of the hall. A deposit of silt between the hearths indicated that the fire position had been reinstated several times after flooding. The topmost hearth was constructed of roofing tiles laid on edge, still covered with charcoal. The surrounding floor was of tamped chalk. At Ludgershall Castle a 'vast hearth of edge-set tiles' was excavated.

At Gomeldon, longhouses of both the twelfth and early fourteenth centuries had hearths against the cross-passage wall. In the first case the wall may have been of mud and stud and burned down, in the second it was a low stone wall. At Littlecote a longhouse had a stone-tiled hearth in a secondary stage of the building. Hearths found during building work have sometimes been large circular stones, for example West End Farm, Urchfont; and Coombe Farm, Axford, Ramsbury. At 5 High Street, Upavon, a fifteenth-century house, a patch of chalky, clay soil intermixed with charcoal was found in the hall close to the centre of a partition wall.

Louvres — Many structures for supporting louvres or chimney pots have been found in Wiltshire roofs. Ceramic louvres were made at pottery kilns in about 1250–1425 and varied from vented ridge tiles to elaborate tiered structures. Several have been excavated from the kiln sites of Nash Hill, Lacock and Laverstock, and one was excavated at Budbury, Bradford-on-Avon (WAM 65). They have knob finials and four or more triangular or circular openings with baffle plates. The diameter of the louvres is about 0.5 m.

On some grand houses, for example Porch House, Potterne, louvres were constructed with horizontal wooden slats, sometimes closed with a rope like a Venetian blind. On lesser houses, old barrels may have been used as chimneys, as they were elsewhere.

Ceramic chimney pots as distinct from louvres were a South of England feature from the thirteenth century onwards. Many were excavated at the Laverstock kilns near Salisbury. They are up to 0.4 m tall and tapered at the top. One is shaped like a castle tower. A drawing of Wilton in about 1568 shows chimney pots on the roof slopes of most of the single-storey houses, with no chimney stacks visible.

Several of the houses in the Close at Salisbury investigated by the Royal Commission on Historical Monuments offer good evidence of louvred constructions on the roof. The Old Deanery has possibly the only thirteenth-century louvre opening surviving in England and another of the fifteenth century. Hemingsby has one against the north wall of the hall and the Abbot of Sherborne's house (Salisbury Museum) has a fifteenth-century example half-way along the three-bay hall roof. All these louvre openings and others found in the county vary in their carpentry details. At Great Porch, Devizes, there is a very large structure half-way along the hall roof for venting the smoke, amounting to a kind of smoke hood, and there was also a small vent in the rear slope of the roof. Evidence for louvres has also been found at 21 Church Street, Lacock; Priory Farm, Axford, Ramsbury; Church Farm, Wingfield; and Robin Cottage, Tisbury, among others. Sometimes two adjacent trusses were plastered over down to the level of the eaves. This was perhaps the case at the George and Dragon Inn, Potterne.

These louvre constructions can be detected by changes in the pattern of the common rafters, with trimmers shortening their length just below the apex of the roof or by changes in the level of the purlins or collars. At Linfurlong, Rowde, where the original thatch remains, there seems to be a deliberate attempt to use a plant with finer stems where the smoke filtered out near the gable end over the inner room (*no. 49*). At the same house there is also a fairly large louvre base in the hall roof. At 8 St John's Street, Devizes, the fifteenth-century louvre base is a compact arrangement about 0.3 m square (*no. 50*).

No. 50 Base of smoke louvre made with slightly curved timbers at 8 St John's Street, Devizes.

No. 49 Base of smoke louvre and thatch of fine-stemmed plants at Linfurlong, Rowde. The thatch is on original riven oak laths.

Smoke-blackening in the roof — Encrusted soot from a former open fire glitters on roof timbers in torch-light. It varies from a slight deposit to an incrustation up to 2.5 cm thick. Noting the variations in deposit along a roof and on different sides of the timbers will often reveal the position of the hearth and is a guide to where evidence of a louvre may be found. If the timbers are only stained black, the room may have had an open fire for only a short period, or a charcoal-burning brazier may have been used. A small area of blackening may be the result of leakage from a smoke bay or timber-framed fireplace (sixteenth or early seventeenth-century features). Misleading staining can also be caused by water penetration or wood beetle treatment. Charring from an accidental fire leaves a distinctive gnawed edge and may affect only part of a timber. Medieval oak can be a surprisingly new-looking grey-brown colour if it has been sealed from the weather and no smoke has reached it.

Fireplaces — Most fireplaces to be seen today in medieval houses are later additions, occasionally of the sixteenth but more often of the seventeenth century or later. Fireplaces were used in castles from the early Middle Ages as it was impractical to have open fires in storeyed buildings. They were usually quite small in size and built in the thickness of the wall. A fireplace is recorded to have been put into the Queen's chamber at Devizes Castle in 1256. The Great Chamber at Old Sarum had a fireplace with a rounded back which was set with tiles in 1366. Another fireplace there had a stone kerb, a rounded back and side pilasters to carry a hood. Some fireplaces of the fourteenth or early fifteenth centuries have been recorded in Wiltshire, mostly in ecclesiastical or manorial buildings. One of the best preserved is in the solar at Daubeney's Farm, Colerne (no. 51), and probably dates from about 1400. The mutilated first-floor fireplace at Castle Cottage, Great Bedwyn, is very similar in its overall shape and cornice. The hood of the ground-floor fireplace at the Bell Inn, Malmesbury (part of the Abbey buildings), protrudes slightly more sharply into the room and may have been supported on shafts. It too has a cornice at the top of the hood. Another fireplace at the inn (no. 52), on the first floor, has the remnants of moulded or shafted jambs. The fireplace at Chantry Cottage, North Wraxall, has unusual rounded shoulders (no. 53).

A greater number of fireplaces survives from the fifteenth century. Most are of larger size than the early examples and have huge lintel stones and moulded Tudor arches. There may be a moulded cornice above, sometimes returned round to the side of the stack. The parlour fireplace at Porch House, Potterne (no. 54), is fairly typical,

No. 51 Fireplace of about 1400 at Daubeney's, Colerne. An inscribed date of 1390, though rare, may be authentic.

No. 52 Mutilated fireplace at the Bell Inn, Malmesbury, formerly the Abbey guesthouse.

No. 53 Solar fireplace at Chantry Cottage, North Wraxall, a cruck-built building, probably of the early fourteenth century, converted to stone around 1400.

No. 54 Parlour fireplace of about 1470 at Porch House, Potterne.

and there are very similar fireplaces at Corbetts Cottage, Castle Combe; in the solar at Black Barn Farm, Steeple Ashton; and from the hall at Bewley Court, Lacock.

Some fifteenth-century fireplaces have square heads. A fireplace at the Court House, Castle Combe, is unusual in design (*no. 55*). At the end of the fifteenth century, more decorated examples with panelling or cusping were made. The fireplace at the Hall of John Hall, Salisbury, is one of the most elaborate. The hall chamber fireplace at 99 High Street, Marlborough, has an overmantel with a panel of tracery. Another from the Prior's Lodging at Bradenstoke Priory (WAM 43) was moved to St Donat's Castle, Glamorgan, by W.R. Hearst, the newspaper millionaire, in the 1920s. Another very attractive example was at the Green Dragon Inn, Alderbury (*no. 56*). One at Gaston Manor, Tisbury (*no. 57*), dates from about 1500, as does a hall fireplace with recessed traceried corner panels in the jambs at Iford Manor, Westwood.

No. 55 *Square-headed fireplace at the Court House, Castle Combe, with a nineteenth-century hob-grate inside.*

No. 56 *Old photograph of a late fifteenth-century fireplace at the Green Dragon Inn, Alderbury, a hall and cross-wing house with a smoke-blackened roof. The building probably belonged to Ivychurch Priory.*

No. 57 *Fireplace of about 1500 at Gaston Manor, Tisbury, with adjoining doorway to a former staircase.*

At the end of the fifteenth and into the sixteenth centuries there were also plainer fireplaces with deeply chamfered or hollow moulded surrounds, but the more intricately moulded surrounds continued to be built.

Fireplace positions — When a fireplace was inserted in the sixteenth or seventeenth centuries into an open hall, it was often put where the hearth had been. Where this was central in a two-bay hall, as at Parks Court, Upton Scudamore; and Great Porch, Devizes, the opportunity was often taken to divide the hall into two rooms with back-to-back fireplaces, and to ceil over the rooms forming chambers above, thus making four rooms where there had been one. Where the hearth had been backing on to the cross-passage the fireplace usually followed, and where it had been close to the parlour or inner room partition as it often was in the east of the county, the fireplace again usually followed. Some cases are known where the fireplace was put in a completely new position, probably because of a greater change in room plan.

No. 58 *Pinnacle chimney of about 1400 at Daubeney's, Colerne.*

No. 59 *Lower part of a pinnacle chimney at Chantry Cottage, North Wraxall.*

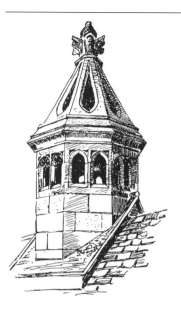

Fig. 15 Octagonal hall chimney at Place House, Tisbury, from an article by P.M. Johnson in Country Life, May 1919.

No. 60 Cylindrical chimney at Castle Cottage, Great Bedwyn (see also no. 4). An eighteenth-century print shows a tapered section above the collar.

No. 61 Square crenellated hall chimney at Easton Court Farm, Easton, Corsham. The fireplace was inserted into an open hall of about 1400.

Chimneys — A number of pinnacle chimneys survive in the county. The most complete is probably the one at Daubeney's, Colerne (*no. 58*). This type is probably related to the wooden louvres which preceded it and acts like a finial at the gable end of the roof. Often the pinnacle itself has gone as it has at Chantry Cottage, North Wraxall (*no. 59*). Another pinnacle chimney is on the gatehouse at Church Farm, Lower Seagry. A more elaborate and possibly later example is the chimney of Place Farmhouse, Tisbury (*fig. 15*). An interesting example, now gone, was on the Red Lion Inn, Corsham (*frontispiece*).

Where a chimney was installed in a lateral position on the side of a house, it needed to be taller to take the smoke above the level of the ridge. A cylindrical chimney was then used. This form was used in castles and important houses from the mid-twelfth century. An ornate example dating from about 1130, with circular smoke-holes and bands of decoration including chevron moulding, was excavated at the King's House, Old Sarum. The cylindrical chimney at Castle Cottage, Great Bedwyn (*no. 60*), may date from about 1400 (comparing the related fireplace with the fireplace and roof at Daubeney's). The cylindrical chimney at Bewley Court, probably built in the 1390s, has a moulded top. It is possible that these chimneys were originally capped by pinnacles. A stage with openings above the top moulding remains at South Wraxall Manor.

Another type, possibly fifteenth century, was the square crenellated chimney. The hall chimney at Great Chalfield Manor is of this type on a tall shaft. Another early square chimney is at Easton Court Farm, Corsham (*no. 61*). There is a polygonal, crenellated chimney on the outer gatehouse at Place Farm, Tisbury (no. 20). A square chimney with two tiers of openings is shown on an old print of Castle Combe (*fig. 13*). The chimney on the inner gatehouse at Place Farm, Tisbury, has a moulded capping carved with paterae, thought to date from the late fifteenth century.

Staircases

In medieval houses the hall was usually open to the apex of the roof, so a staircase would only be needed, for example, to a gallery over a screens passage, a solar or great chamber or in a lesser house to a loft over the inner room or the service end. First-floor halls had external stone staircases, but in other stone houses of high status, staircases were usually built spirally in the thickness of the wall or next to a chimney stack (*no. 57*). Frequently a more imposing staircase was built in the sixteenth century or later, and only a circular section of wall shows where the early stair was. Bewley Court, Lacock, is unusual in having a wide, straight flight of stone steps in an area alongside the hall (*fig. 16*). This is more like the staircases of cathedral buildings and monasteries where such space could be afforded. Sometimes, as at The Chantry, Mere; and Great

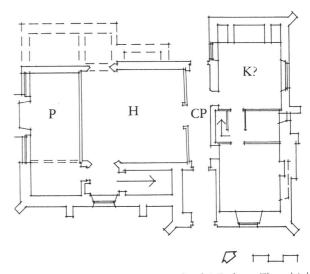

Fig. 16 Plan of Bewley Court, Lacock, based on that of H. Brakspear. The porch is largely within the house and the staircase is to the side.

Porch, Devizes, the door to the stair led off the cross-passage, but if the stair was a timber construction the actual steps have usually been replaced. There are, apparently, no known medieval timber staircases in Wiltshire. They must usually have been quite steep, as only small areas are available. Sometimes an original first-floor doorway suggests a stair in the corner of the hall. Possibly it was a ladder with rungs or with flat steps. Future study of pegholes in adjacent timbers may supply some answers.

Partitions

Partition walls may be of stone in a stone house or of timber framing in either a stone or a timber house. Framing is infilled with wattle and daub and the partition wall is usually beneath a closed roof truss. The framing pattern of partition walls can differ from that of the outside walls of the same house. While the panels of an outside wall may be positioned to accommodate windows, those inside the house may have only doorways. (*no. 62*).

Sometimes in fifteenth-century houses, plank-and-muntin partitions are found alongside a cross-passage. This is the case at the Woodhouse, St Mary Street, Chippenham (*no. 63*), and at the King and Queen Inn, Highworth.

Screens

The great halls of large houses often had screens of timber or stone, separating the hall from the cross-passage and supporting a gallery

No. 62 End frame with the panels spaced to incorporate a central window at first-floor level. The partition frame at the opposite end of the room has a central post instead. 63 Fore Street, Trowbridge.

No. 63 Plank-and-muntin partition at the Woodhouse, St Mary Street, Chippenham.

above. At Great Chalfield the elaborately carved oak screen was drawn in the nineteenth century and a copy was later made. There is evidence for a stone screen at Bewley Court. At Hemingsby, The Close, Salisbury, some reset doorways with low, four-centred heads and flanking crocketed standards survive from the screen. Talboys, Keevil, still has a timber gallery, but this has possibly been repositioned (*no. 1*).

Internal jetties, coving and dais benches

As the upper part of the hall was not normally lofted, extra space was sometimes put into adjacent first-floor rooms by jettying them over the hall. This is described as an internal jetty. At Big Thatch, Ford, North Wraxall, a solar over a low 'cellar' or store-room was inserted in the fifteenth century into a cruck-built house which had previously had an inner room open to the roof in that position. The new solar was jettied over the hall (*no. 64*) and a dais bench for the head of the household was fixed below it. The jetty was therefore rather like the dais canopy found in some parts of England. At Trunnell's Farm, Colerne, it is the room over the cross-passage that is jettied over the hall (*no. 65*). At Bewley Court, Lacock, the Great Chamber in the cross-wing is jettied over the cross-passage with stone coving underneath (*no. 35*).

The fixed bench in the hall served the high table. A wall with a stone bench survives in the thirteenth century hall at Old Sarum. Fixing points for timber benches are fairly often found when buildings are recorded, but it is rare for any of the bench to remain.

No. 64 Internal jetty at Big Thatch, Ford, North Wraxall. When the hall was ceiled in the seventeenth century, additional posts were put under the jetty and another above to support the new ceiling beam. The shaped end of a bench can be seen under the right-hand jetty joist.

Beams and joists

Some early beams in Wiltshire have very deep chamfers (15 cm, or even more) without stops. More often in the fifteenth century, beams were heavily moulded, and the joists between were moulded to match (*no. 66*). Another decoration involved a carved boss at the intersection of moulded beams (*no. 67*). Many fairly small houses at Steeple Ashton, and in other communities made richer through the cloth trade, have ceilings of this kind. They were still being constructed with slightly different mouldings in the sixteenth century. In a few cases where no expense was spared, the ceiling was divided into small panels enriched with many carvings. The

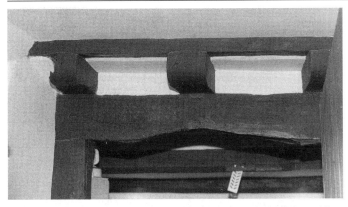

No. 65 Internal jetty over the mutilated doorway from the cross-passage, Trunnell's Farm, Colerne.

No. 66 Ceiling with a moulded beam and moulded joists, Edington Farm, Edington.

parlour at Talboys, Keevil (*no. 68*), is a good example of this. Usually it was the parlour that had moulded beams. Great Chalfield is unusual in having a hall lofted over and its ceiling has moulded beams with bosses. In the medieval period, joists were of heavier timber than in later centuries and were always laid flat, that is with the widest dimension horizontal.

Squints

At Great Chalfield there are squint windows in the form of masks, giving a view into the hall. Other squints have been found at the Old Vicarage, Steeple Ashton; and at Porch House, Potterne.

Lavers

In the Middle Ages, people ate mainly with their fingers and water containers were often provided either as a vessel on the table or as a fixture built into a nearby wall. The best example in Wiltshire is at Easton Court Farm, Corsham (*no. 69*). This may date from the late fifteenth century as it is in the side of a fireplace stack inserted into an open hall at that time. It has a lower shelf at one side, perhaps for a cloth, and no drain. An alcove at the Court House, Castle Combe (*no. 70*), may also be a laver. At Sheldon Manor in the accounts of 1431 concerning the building of the solar cross-wing, there is a mention of 'one drain length 20 feet'. There is still a stone cistern on the cross-passage side of the thick dividing wall between the hall and the cross-wing, with a wooden drainpipe leading down to it (*no. 71*).

No. 67 *Moulded beams of about 1500 with a boss of carved leaves. Dial House, Seend.*

No. 69 *Laver for washing hands in the side of the hall fireplace stack at Easton Court Farm, Easton, Corsham.*

No. 70 *Possible laver at the Court House, Castle Combe.*

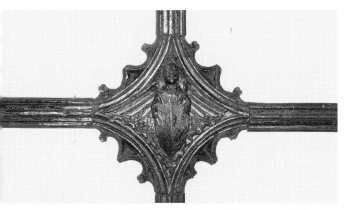

No. 68 *Boss with a carved angel holding a shield from the intricately panelled parlour ceiling at Talboys, Keevil.*

No. 71 Stone cistern and wooden pipe leading down to it from the roof, probably of 1431, in the cross-passage at Sheldon Manor, Chippenham Without.

No. 72 Pair of wall cupboards at the foot of the stairs outside the room that may have been the chapel at Bewley Court, Lacock.

Wall cupboards

Very few original medieval cupboards survive. There are several at Bewley Court, Lacock. A pair are set at the foot of the staircase (*no. 72*) and two more, of L-shaped plan, are next to the Great Chamber fireplace. It is possible that they were used for deeds, valuables or chapel items.

Lighting

Occasionally, evidence of the position of lights can be seen. At Dauntsey Park, Dauntsey, on one of the base-cruck roof trusses, there is the mark of a taper burn and a group of nails which may have supported a light (*no. 73*). The risk of fire is obvious.

No. 73 Group of nails in a base cruck and a related taper burn mark, suggesting the position of a light. Dauntsey Park, Dauntsey.

Wall-paintings and furnishings

Some ways in which medieval houses were ornamented have already been mentioned and the decorative features of roofs are discussed below. However, the richer houses were full of further colour and decoration from paint, fittings and furnishings.

In the thirteenth century, wall plaster was sometimes painted with red lines to look like ashlar masonry. This was the case at the Old Deanery, Salisbury. At Leadenhall, also in the Close, at each crossing of the red lines there was a calyx of four small black leaves. From each alternate one issued to right and left a black stem with a flower of five red petals and a white centre, so that there was a flower in each compartment of the trellis. An old postcard shows the hall walls of Talboys, Keevil, with a scattered floral pattern. The George Inn at Trowbridge had a first-floor chamber with a chequer pattern, which may have been medieval, continuing over the timber framing. There were flowers painted at the junctions of the chequers. Great Porch, Devizes, has at roof level the remnants of the hall's painting of large flowers and foliage (*no. 74*). Some rooms seem to have been painted a single colour, usually red ochre. Traces have been found, for example, in the hall of Hemingsby at Salisbury and in the front chamber of 63 Fore Street, Trowbridge. Painted pictures were sometimes included as part of an overall pattern. At Talboys there is the picture of a talbot (possibly a Garter symbol) in the hall and there were bestiary paintings in the parlour of which an elephant and castle (*no. 75*) and a possible unicorn survive. Domestic chapels probably often had wall-paintings. There was a large mural of St Christopher in the chapel room of the Rogers' manor house at Bradford-on-Avon.

No. 74 Floral wall-painting on the end-wall of the hall at Great Porch, Devizes.

Furnishings

The 1418 inventory of Bewley Court (WAM 81) gives a good idea of the colours of the furnishings of a rich house. In the Great Chamber there was a great red bed, one coverlet, the tester of tapestry work of the arms of Chelrey (Calston's wife's family), one canopy, three curtains of red worsted and six cushions with the Chelrey arms. In the parlour chamber there was a white bed 'powdered' with red garlands of roses, and blue and green curtains. In the hall of this house the side-walls have two slightly sunken panels outlined with roll moulding which may have held wall-paintings or hangings (*no. 2*).

No. 75 Wall-painting of an elephant and castle in the parlour at Talboys, Keevil.

Roof Structure

The roof is often the most intact part of a medieval house. Its construction required many different timbers and joints, therefore there are a large number of roof features that can be found in different combinations. Controlling factors were fashion, the size and lengths of timber available and the plan of the house.

Medieval roof trusses can be 'open' or 'closed'. An open truss is not part of a partition. It spans an open room and therefore has no infill material and fewer strengthening timbers forming a frame. Tiebeams at the level of the eaves were rarely used in open trusses. As it is in a prominent position and usually in a reception room, an open truss can be used to display wealth by the richness of its carpentry. Being more elaborate, open trusses have more often been illustrated in books. The closed trusses which accompany them may be simpler but related in form, or may be very different.

The roofs of medieval timber houses in Wiltshire are of two basic types: cruck construction where the walls and roof are framed in one, or post and truss with a vertical post in the wall jointed to a separate roof truss. Many fragments of archaic roofs from before 1300 survive as reused timbers in the roofs of Wiltshire houses and would merit future study.

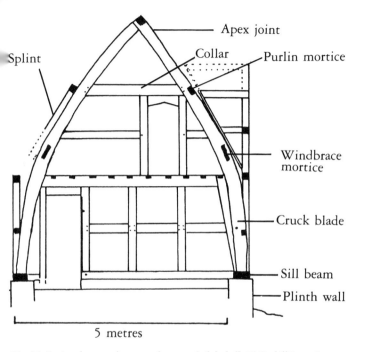

Splint

Apex joint

Collar — Purlin mortice

Windbrace mortice

Cruck blade

Sill beam

Plinth wall

5 metres

Fig. 17 Section of true-cruck truss at the west end of the hall, 10 Coxhill Lane, Potterne. The first floor over the inner room may be original, but the dormer window is a later addition.

Crucks

Cruck-built houses are probably the most common surviving medieval buildings in the county. With a few exceptions, two types of cruck were used: base crucks and true crucks (*fig. 17*). About twelve base-cruck houses still exist or are known to have existed and about 134 true-cruck houses remain. The base-cruck buildings were of very high status, usually manor houses or the capital messuages of freehold estates. They tend to be earlier in date than surviving true-cruck buildings. Base crucks have a scattered distribution but houses with true crucks are distributed all over the county with some concentration in the west central area. More of both types are still being discovered. True-cruck houses may be clustered in groups, for example twelve at Lacock, five at Salisbury, Steeple Ashton and Urchfont and four at Devizes, Chiseldon and Potterne. Eight parishes have three cruck houses, fifteen have two and forty-six have one. In at least five cases there are cruck houses on neighbouring plots or across the road from each other, suggesting the possibility of a laid-out, planted manorial development. Lacock High Street is the best example. Where there are houses with crucks there are often also barns or other farm buildings of cruck construction. Twenty-three of these are known to exist.

Wiltshire crucks are found in both towns and villages. Many are situated in manors owned by ecclesiastical authorities: Lacock (Lacock Abbey), Potterne and Bishops Cannings (Salisbury Cathedral), Steeple Ashton (Romsey Abbey, Hampshire), Melksham (Canons of Salisbury Cathedral), Chiseldon (Hyde Abbey) and Bremhill (Malmesbury

No. 76 *Unusually wavy cruck-blade at 3 Church Street, Lacock. The cruck spur at the level of the eaves, which once supported a wall-post, is visible.*

Abbey). The tenant usually arranged and paid for the building of the house but the substantial oak trunks for crucks were probably granted by the landowner. This was an investment as cruck-built houses are particularly long-lasting. Timbers for post and truss houses are of a smaller size and were therefore more easily found.

The characteristics of Wiltshire true-cruck trusses — One side of a cruck truss is called a blade or simply a cruck, (not a 'cruck beam' as a beam is a horizontal timber). A cruck-blade is wider and often thicker than a wall-post, providing better support for the

wall and roof and eliminating the potentially weak joint between the post and the roof truss (*no. 76*). The side-walls can easily be replaced by different materials as they decay. The best crucks of heart wood are usually reserved for each end of the hall and its central open truss if the hall is two bays long. The blades are about 0.4 m wide at the elbow and the blade usually curves slightly to the elbow with a fairly straight profile above that level. In a few cases there is a gradual curve from the foot to the apex. There is usually a mortice at the elbow for a cruck spur to join the blade to a wall-post behind. There are usually mortices at a slightly higher level for at least one tier of wind-braces, but the wind-braces sometimes crossed over on the back of the blade and were secured by a nail to either the blade or a packing piece of timber behind it. Wiltshire crucks usually have a collar between the blades above elbow level, often arch-braced, but do not normally have original tie beams attached by a lap joint. Several crucks at Lacock are an exception. Lap-jointed tie beams in the end-walls are found extensively in the Midlands and elsewhere. Because of their inward curve, crucks were not suitable for fully two-storeyed buildings. Wiltshire cruck houses all originally had the hall open to the roof with no first-floor chamber above.

Where the blades join at the apex, various forms of joint were used, some of which were widely used in England and some of which are local (*fig. 21*). Different apex joints were often used in one building, apparently in order to make use of different lengths of cruck blades and still position the ridge-piece at the same height along the roof. Usually the blades were a matching pair from one tree cut in half, but if they did not match and one blade was not sufficiently long, a section of timber was scarfed onto the top. This is called an extended cruck and examples have been seen at Devizes, Potterne and Bishops Cannings.

The plans of true-cruck houses — Cruck houses are usually three-bays long with a three-room and cross-passage plan (*fig. 6*). The passage can be either in the hall bay or in the services bay. Sometimes they have only two bays with just a hall and an inner room, but an original service end may have been lost. The house was usually built entirely of crucks. Where there is a post and truss cross-wing it is normally an addition of the fifteenth or sixteenth century.

Fig. 18 The black area of England and Wales shows where true-cruck houses had been found by 1981 (based on the Cruck Catalogue).

The origins and distribution of crucks — Crucks are found in the western, central and northern parts of England and in most of Wales, but are totally absent from the east of England, Cornwall and Pembrokeshire (*fig. 18*). They are also found in Ireland, Scotland, parts of France, Italy, the Low Countries, Germany, Eastern Europe and Denmark. Such a wide distribution suggests an early origin. Sloping wall timbers were used in England during the Roman occupation in the third and fourth centuries. Use during the Saxon period is disputed, but excavations show that crucks were certainly employed by the late eleventh or early twelfth century. Documentary evidence from other areas mentions crucks, sometimes called siles or forks, from the late twelfth century onwards. One of the earliest excavated sites is at Gomeldon in Wiltshire (see p. 18). Tree-ring dating has shown that surviving true crucks in the south of England can date back to the late thirteenth century and were being built until the very end of the fifteenth century. In the North Midlands, further north and in Ireland their use in single-storey cottages continued into the early seventeenth century.

The problem in finding very early examples from excavation is that the crucks were set directly into the ground in postholes and if the feet of the blades rise vertically at first they are indistinguishable from wall-posts. Recent re-interpretation by Stuart Wrathmell, of excavations at Wharram Percy in Yorkshire and on Dartmoor, shows that the stone walls of early houses were often replacements of earlier timber walls between crucks. The crucks continued to be used, often with the rotted feet cut off and set on low walls and the walls might be rebuilt a number of times on slightly different alignments. The original postholes became sealed underneath and appear, wrongly, to belong to an earlier house, the superstructure of which has gone. It used to be thought that early medieval houses were impermanent and rebuilt each generation but they were probably as well built as late medieval houses and with repair lasted hundreds of years.

Wiltshire crucks may have originally had their feet set into the ground. Wick Cottage, Heddington (no. 33), a house at Bemerton and a cruck barn of 1484–5 at Bremhill still have crucks directly on or in the ground. It must certainly have been easier to rear a cruck truss by dropping it into postholes than by raising it up onto a wall or boulders. Plinth walls of heights up to about 0.9 m are found, but without excavation it is impossible to tell whether they are original. The process of progressively cutting off the feet of crucks can still be seen today during building work.

The evidence for earlier timber walls in cruck buildings — Most cruck houses in Wiltshire still retain some timber framing. Where crucks and base crucks are set in stone or flint walls, they are described as 'raised' when their feet are between a quarter and half-way up the wall, usually resting on pads. This may not be the original situation. The upper part of the stone wall may be an addition in place of a timber wall. The pads under the crucks are often cut up lengths of the earlier sill beam. Sometimes the stone walls show vertical joints or bulges in the plan outline, suggesting piecemeal infilling in stone around the crucks when framing was removed. Other evidence may lie in a change in the masonry at the level of the pads, with stones of a different type or size or a

different mortar being used above. This is the case at Lacock tithe barn. At Garsdon Manor the walls of the base-cruck range are 'mostly rebuilt or repaired but the lower courses and a mutilated buttress on the south side are apparently medieval'. There may be mortices in the blades for cruck spurs which would have tied them to timber wall-posts, as at the barn at Church Farm, Atworth, and at Bramble Cottage, Preston, Lyneham. However, the absence of cruck spurs may not prove the walls were always stone. The timber-framed base-cruck barn at Cherhill had none, nor does 10 Coxhill Lane, Potterne (fig. 17). Sometimes the stone walls from ground level are a complete rebuilding, as at Dutch Cottage,

No. 77 Dutch Cottage, Chippenham, a cruck house later encased in stone.

82

Chippenham (*no. 77*). They may, by an odd angle with the crucks, show that they were only built when an upper floor was required (*no. 78*). Dendro-dating can be useful and may show that the roof timbers are earlier than wall features. It seems possible that some cruck buildings were thatched at first and when stone-tiled later were reinforced by the replacement of timber walls with buttressed stone walls. Eight samples from the Glastonbury Abbey tithe barn in Somerset were dendro-dated *c.* 1250–1300, with other timbers of 1343–61. Documents show the barn was thatched in 1302/3–1380/1 but was tiled in 1389–90. The stonework has been dated as late fourteenth century. In the clay valleys, cruck houses often had the framing replaced in the eighteenth century by brick.

There are no known cruck houses with cob walls as there are in Somerset and Devon.

The positions where crucks or fragments are found — The following positions of crucks all occur, sometimes several within one house: (a) In the end walls, for example: 3 Church Street, Lacock (*no. 76*); 1 Ball Road, Pewsey; 10 Coxhill Lane, Potterne (*no. 12*); 11 Dark Lane North, Steeple Ashton; Townsend Cottage, Urchfont. (b) The lower parts of the blades are left and the tops cut off when a beam is inserted for a first floor, for example the George and Dragon Inn, Potterne; and the Sanctuary, Steeple Ashton. (c) One or both blades are left embedded in a partition wall or in the front wall of a chimney stack. The apex may be cut off at the level of the eaves or above, and a later roof built at a higher level, for example Thornend Farm, Christian Malford; and 4 and 6 Canon Square, Melksham. (d) The walls are rebuilt and the lower parts of the crucks cut off, but the tops where straight above the elbow are retained as roof principals, sometimes in situ and sometimes dismantled and reused in a new, taller building on the site, for example: 1 and 2 The Parade, Marlborough; Manor House, Steeple Ashton; and Unicorn House, Malmesbury. (e) The straight section above the elbow is re-used as a beam supporting the joists of the attic floor or as a window lintel, for example the George and Dragon Inn, Potterne.

Recognizing crucks re-used as principal rafters or in other positions — The shaping of the timber, narrowing towards the apex and possibly with a slight arc, is the strongest evidence, but other points add weight. For example the position of the collar, usually quite high and the lack of an original tie-beam; trenched purlin mortices, or the lack of purlin mortices because the purlin was on a splint or packing piece behind the cruck; an early apex type; timber looking older than the rest of the roof, smoke-blackened in a clean roof, with redundant windbraces or other mortices showing that it has been re-used.

Jointed crucks — In Ireland, Wales, Devon, Somerset and Dorset, cruck-blades were sometimes made from two timbers jointed at the elbow. This was a useful method in an area without large oaks but it seems also to represent a different tradition of cruck construction. Jointed crucks are normally found in walls of a solid material, cob or stone, and show no evidence for any earlier timber walls. The joints are usually made in one of two ways with pegging from either the front or the side. It is interesting that while the area of jointed crucks extends to the Wiltshire border on the west with many found at Norton St Philip and Beckington, not one normal jointed cruck has been found within Wiltshire. There is a cruck truss at Linfurlong, Rowde (*no. 79*), jointed in a very different way. There are a few unusual outliers too in Oxfordshire and Worcestershire. A few post-and truss fifteenth-century buildings in Wiltshire have a complicated joint between the post- and the truss which also looks slightly related to jointed crucks. Several have been recorded at Westbury.

Upper crucks — Upper crucks occur in two-storey buildings where the crucks rest on a ceiling beam below the top of the walls. Sometimes this may be a re-use of shortened full-length crucks.

No. 79 Jointed cruck showing the joint, pegs and circular carpenter's marks. Linfurlong, Rowde.

No. 80 The jettied New Inn, Salisbury, which also has an internal jetty and an upper cruck truss.

Many upper crucks are listed from other parts of England, but it is not a Wiltshire type. Two apparent instances are: on the service side of the cross-passage at Lower Berrycourt Farm, Donhead St Mary, and at the New Inn, New Street, Salisbury, a jettied structure of suggested late fifteenth-century date (*no. 80* and RCHME '**Salisbury**', p. 78–9).

End crucks — A single end cruck or gavelfork was sometimes used in the centre of the end-wall of a house to support the end of the ridge-piece. This enabled the final pair of ordinary crucks to be placed some way from the end-wall and reduced the number of timbers required. It also tended to result in a boat-shaped building. One end cruck survives in a cottage at Hodson, Chiseldon.

Misleading roof types that may resemble crucks — Readers should beware of knee principals, also known as knee rafters (explained in *Wiltshire Farmhouses and Cottages 1500–1850*, pp. 65–6), which were used in the late seventeenth and eighteenth centuries, and also of sling brace roofs (*Wiltshire Farm Buildings 1500–1900*, pp. 46–7), used in barns, stables and granaries in the eighteenth and early nineteenth centuries. Both of these roof types have curved timbers which superficially resemble crucks. Curved principals are a medieval roof type where the principal rafters have sharply curved feet set just below the level of the eaves in a stone wall. The only recorded Wiltshire example is the central hall truss at Bewley Court, Lacock (*no. 81*).

Base crucks — Base crucks differ from true crucks in rising from either ground level or low walls to the level of a tie, well below the

No. 81   Hall roof with curved principals on stone corbels and apex crucks. Bewley Court, Lacock.

No. 82   Arch-braced tie across a base-cruck truss at Dauntsey Park, Dauntsey. The superstructure, now gone, was probably a pair of apex crucks.

apex, which yokes the tops of the blades together (*no. 82*). Above the tie there can be a variety of different superstructures. The main elements of these are: (a) crown-posts (see also pp. 89–90), (b) a small cruck making with the base crucks a two-tier cruck, (c) coupled rafters, (d) principal rafters and a collar. (a) and (b) can be combined, as at Garsdon Manor (*no. 83*) and Bradenstoke Abbey, or (a) and (c) can be combined, as at Parks Court, Upton Scudamore. (b) is also found in Somerset, Dorset and Gloucestershire. The tie is rather like a heavy collar and is often cranked (angled upwards at the centre), as it is at Fowlswick Farm (*fig. 19*). The superstructure sometimes has an upper collar with rounded arch-bracing, as at the Old Vicarage, Yatton Keynell, or at each side of a strutted crown-post making a pair of pointed arches, as at Bradenstoke Abbey and at the Old Vicarage, Bremhill (*no. 84*).

Wiltshire base crucks seem to date from the period 1250–1350 and include some of the earliest surviving roofs. A base cruck aisled house at Harwell, Oxfordshire has been dendro-dated to the mid-thirteenth century. Base crucks are found in high-status houses, have heavier timbers than true crucks and usually span greater widths. Unlike true crucks they are mixed with other sorts of trusses in the same building. They are generally used for the open trusses of a great hall, with different trusses more like those of aisled halls, being used at the ends of the hall (*no. 85*).

No. 83 Crown-post, collar purlin above and apex crucks at Garsdon Manor, Lea and Cleverton.

No. 84 Top of a base-cruck truss at the Old Vicarage, Bremhill, with arch-bracing and moulded crown-post. A plain crown-post can be seen in the truss in the end-wall. All lighter-coloured timbers are later.

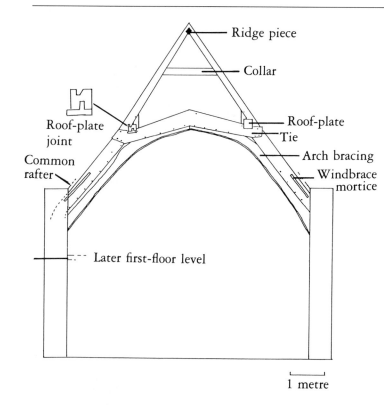

Ridge piece

Collar

Roof-plate

Roof-plate
joint

Tie

Common
rafter

Arch bracing

Windbrace
mortice

Later first-floor level

1 metre

No. 85 Arch-braced tie and the base of the crown-post in the base-cruck truss at Parks Court, Upton Scudamore.

Fig. 19 Section of central base-cruck truss in the hall, Fowlswick Farm, Chippenham Without. The lower parts of the cruck blades were removed when the walls were rebuilt in stone but the start of the curve is visible in the stonework.

Where base crucks are used with posts and trusses, this may indicate the remnants of an older tradition from aisled houses; one preserved in jointed cruck houses in Somerset (VA 22) and elsewhere and seen also in medieval aisled barns in southern England. A barn at Siddington, Gloucestershire, of the mid-thirteenth century has two aisled trusses and two base crucks. The barn at Manor Farm, Cherhill, had the same combination. Base-cruck single-aisled buildings are found in Hampshire and further east, but none are known in Wiltshire.

Base crucks were used for display and the timbers are often moulded or chamfered. Where a small apex cruck was used in combination with a crown-post the truss was more substantial than was needed to support the roof. The carpenter was striving for a deliberate artistic effect combining the elements available in a new, beautiful and impressive way as one might expect in a church roof.

Crown-posts

Crown-posts are posts rising from the centre of a tie-beam, or the tie of a base cruck, which support a collar purlin. The collar purlin in turn supports the collars of trussed rafters all along the roof. Crown posts are plain or octagonal in Wiltshire and may have two-way or four-way struts attached (*no. 86*). They originated in the second half of the thirteenth century, and examples from before 1300 can be found in high-quality buildings in about nine counties of south-east and central England, including Wiltshire. One of the very earliest is at the

No. 86 Plain crown-post in the end-wall of the hall and cut off collar purlin resting on it. Parks Court, Upton Scudamore.

Old Deanery, Salisbury, of about 1258–74. They continued in use in the east of England, especially Kent and East Anglia, until the fifteenth century or even later.

There are crown-posts at the aisled Old House, Market Lavington, of the early fourteenth century. A pair of parallel crown-posts roofs, with timber-framed walls occur at the George Inn, High Street, Salisbury, thought to date from between 1361 and 1379. The crown-posts are short, chamfered and stopped. They lack caps and bases and are in lesser chambers of the inn. The main chamber has an arch-braced roof with ornamental cusping. The only known barn with a crown-post roof in Wiltshire was that at Cherhill. It had a very plain crown-post as was usual in barns, with transverse braces running down from the post to the tie. Crown-posts in early houses usually have four-way braces running upwards. From the late thirteenth century to about 1350 they were often richly ornamented with moulded caps and bases. It was an admired form of roofing and at Bradenstoke Abbey the crown-posts had no structural function as there was no collar purlin. The early fourteenth-century refectory roof had ballflower ornament on the arch-braces, an octagonal crown-post with moulded cap and base, its own collar and lateral braces. Crown-posts are also used with

base crucks at the Old Vicarage Bremhill (*nos. 84 and 87*); Parks Court, Upton Scudamore (*no. 85*); and Garsdon Manor, Lea and Cleverton (*no. 83*). The Garsdon crown-posts are short and plain. At Bradenstoke and Garsdon there are also small 'apex crucks' making two tiers of crucks. This combination with crown-posts is only found in Wiltshire and Somerset. At Salisbury there are a number of other examples of crown-posts. At Balles Place a crown-post surmounted a fourteenth-century hammer-beam roof (WAM 59). Mercer suggests that the fashion for columnar decoration gave way to one for panelled decoration and so displaced crown-posts.

Trussed-rafter roofs

A crown-post with an attached collar purlin running along the length of the roof was designed to support trussed rafters, that is pairs of common rafters with a collar near the apex of each pair to strengthen them. The late thirteenth-century Guildhall at Salisbury, shown in old prints, had a roof of this type, and so has Garsdon Manor (*no. 83*). Sometimes trussed-rafter roofs had no strengthening collar purlin or crown-post at the end of the bay, but were strengthened by arch-bracing to each pair of rafters. The porch roof of Sheldon Manor, Chippenham Without, possibly of the late thirteenth century, is of this type (*no. 88*), and so is the porch roof of Woodlands Manor, Mere. Sometimes there are timber upright supports called ashlaring at the eaves. A cross-wing of Old Manor, West Lavington, has a larger roof of similar construction.

No. 87 Detail of the octagonal moulded crown-post at the Old Vicarage, Bremhill.

No. 88 Trussed-rafter roof with arch-bracing, over the porch at Sheldon Manor, Chippenham Without.

Hammer-beam and false hammer-beam trusses

A hammer-beam roof designed for a stone vault was depicted in the early thirteenth century, but they were most popular in the mid- to late fourteenth century. In the fifteenth century the trusses were decorated with cusping and tracery. The best-known example in England is Westminster Hall, built between 1394 and 1401, with stone walls and a 20.7 m width. The hammer-beam suits open trusses and was particularly used in churches. A few are found in the medieval houses of Wiltshire. One of the earliest, simple yet impressive, is at 9 Queen Street, Salisbury, of about 1306. An ornate fifteenth-century example is the hall roof at Porch House, Potterne (*no. 89*). Some other examples are at Balles Place, the Plume of Feathers Inn, and Windover House (a friary), at Salisbury. False hammer-beam roofs with the stump of a tie-beam at the foot of an arch-braced collar truss are more common. The fifteenth-century oratory roof of the Chantry, 99 High Street, Marlborough, is of this type. Others occur in the cross-wing of the Sanctuary, Steeple Ashton, and at the late fifteenth-century Hall of John Hall, also at Salisbury. In a chamber of The George Inn at Salisbury and in the hall of South Wraxall Manor, carved heads, shields or grotesque animals decorate the false hammer-beams.

Arch-braced collar trusses

The arch-braced collar roof was an extremely common roof type in Wiltshire and was a logical development from arch-braced base crucks and full crucks when two-storey post-and-truss buildings took over. The type originated in the fourteenth century but most

No. 89 Hammer-beam in the hall roof at Porch House, Potterne. A moulded wall-plate runs along behind it.

No. 90 Heavily smoke-blackened hall roof of Axford Farm, Ramsbury.

local examples date from the fifteenth or sixteenth centuries. It was a sturdy construction used in both stone and timber buildings and was strong enough to support a stone-tiled roof. The trusses could be placed close together if desired or there could be intermediate trusses of less strength between them. The roof type was suitable for open trusses and could also be used against, or about one foot inside, a stone end-wall. The upper rooms were open to the roof and the arch-bracing and wind-braces formed patterns. Above the collar there were sometimes V struts (*no. 90*), especially in the early and mid-fifteenth century.

Collar and tie-beam trusses

The collar and tie-beam truss was especially used for closed (infilled) positions in end-walls and partitions (*no. 23*) and was often used in combination with arch-braced collar trusses. It became the predominant type in the post-medieval period when houses were floored throughout. Quite often there is an additional upper collar, a central strut, a pair of queen struts or braces within the truss. An unusual use in a three-bay smoke-blackened open hall occurs at 11 Silver Street, Bradford-on-Avon (WAM 80), perhaps of about 1400, where the tie-beam and collar are both arch-braced.

Scissor and scissor-braced trusses

The open trusses of 52–54 High Street, Salisbury (Beach's Bookshop), are very unusual scissor trusses of the fourteenth century. The principal rafters cross near the apex with short, straight upper principals above. Scissor braces are used at the Plume of Feathers Inn and the Red Lion Inn, Milford Street, also in Salisbury. Three fifteenth-century examples of scissor-bracing have been recorded in the west of the county at the Woodhouse, Chippenham, and at 48 and 38 High Street, Steeple Ashton (*no. 91*). This roof type gave almost as much headroom on an upper floor as an arch-braced collar truss, but was even more impressive.

Principal rafters

Principal rafters are sometimes chamfered in good-quality houses. At Apshill House, Lower Chicksgrove, Tisbury, they are

No. 91 Scissor-braced truss at 38 High Street, Steeple Ashton. A simpler collar and tie-beam closed truss can be seen in the end-wall.

hollow-chamfered with the moulding continued along the collar. At Place Farm, Tisbury, they are cusped. Sometimes there is subtle shaping under the apex which may match shaping of the arch-bracing.

Collars and arch-bracing

The collars and arch-bracing are often the focus of much decoration. The arch-bracing is frequently moulded (*no. 92*). It may be in two sections (called double arch-braced) with the bottom section continuing some feet down the wall. At Talboys it continues down to sill-beam level as a shaft with a cap and base (*no. 93*). The arch-bracing can be cusped, as at Cloately Manor (*fig. 20*).

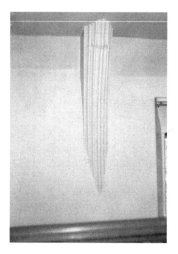

No. 92 Moulded arch-brace visible on the landing at Axford Farm, Ramsbury.

No. 93 Hall window with shafts supporting arch-bracing at each side. The window is a nineteenth-century restoration. Talboys, Keevil.

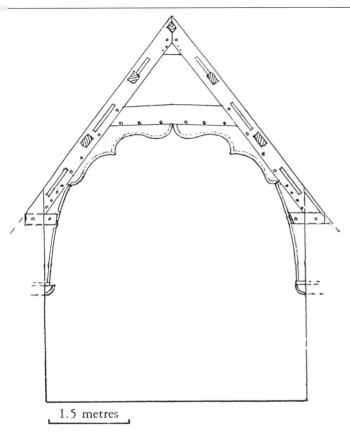

1.5 metres

Fig. 20 Cloately Manor, Hankerton, section through the west wing, based with permission on a drawing by the RCHME. The spurs at the level of the eaves and other features suggest the walls were originally timber-framed.

No. 94 Heavily carved boss at the junction of the arch-bracing on the hall truss. Axford Farm, Ramsbury (see no. 90). All the exposed faces are carved.

At Daubeney's, Colerne, it runs down to the solar floor where there are broach stops. The arch-bracing may be solid at the spandrels (*nos. 82 and 90*) or open. Where the two sides meet at the collar it may join onto a block, pendant from the collar or a carved boss (*nos. 90 and 94*). Where the arch-bracing has gone, its position can be deduced from a series of peg-holes and mortices in the principal rafter or cruck and in the collar.

Apex types

Medieval houses have a greater variety of apex types than later houses and new ones are continually being discovered. Some of those shown in the national *Cruck Catalogue* have been recorded in Wiltshire in cruck and non-cruck buildings, and a number of additional local types (*fig. 21*). It is more common for the ridge-piece to be set diagonally than flat. Where the ridge-piece is clasped it is often difficult to see the joint above it. P1 like this occurs in the thirteenth-century roof at Fowlswick Farm. Dating is as yet very tentative. Possible fourteenth-century types are B2, C2, C3, F4, F5, F7, N1, N2 and N3 (*no. 95*). Late fourteenth to fifteenth-century types may be A1, B1, M2 and P2. Fifteenth-century types may be D1, M1 and M3. Late fifteenth-century and later types may be C1, E1, F6, M4 and Q1 (*no. 96*). The *Cruck Catalogue* also has F1, F2, F3, G, H, K, L1 and L2. K is C1 over an apex cruck, L1 is A1 with a block under the apex and L2 is B1 with a block under the apex. Blocks were sometimes used in Wiltshire as in *fig. 20* which shows M2 with a block. Apex crucks in Wiltshire use a variety of apex types, not just C1.

No. 95 Apex type N3 to a cruck truss at Wick Cottage, Heddington. There is plastered wattle-and-daub infilling between this truss and an adjoining taller cruck truss seen to the right.

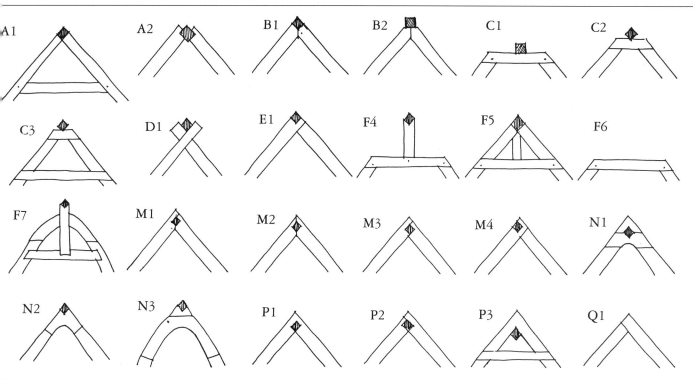

Fig. 21 Some apex-types used in medieval Wiltshire roofs.

Wall-plates

The wall-plate runs along the top of the wall supporting the common rafters. A cornice is sometimes attached. In the fifteenth century they were often elaborately moulded (*no. 97*). Sometimes they were panelled with carved tracery (*no. 98*) or they were castellated. At Great Porch, Devizes at the base of the intermediate trusses, carved heads are attached to the wall-plate (*no. 99*).

No. 97 Moulded wall-plate at Talboys, Keevil

No. 96 Apex type Q1 with no ridge-piece at 35–36 The Temple, Corsley, a cottage. This is the top of a cruck truss infilled with wattle and daub.

No. 98 Panelled wall-plate with carved tracery at 4 St John's Court, Devizes, a stone house which belonged to Thomas Coventry, mayor in 1430. It was left to the town in his will of 1451 to support new almshouses.

No. 99 *Carved head, perhaps depicting the owner, at Great Porch, Devizes.*

Purlins and roof-plates

The term 'side purlin' is used in the east of England to distinguish them from collar purlins. In Wiltshire where collar purlins are comparitively rare, those along the sides of the roof are simply called 'purlins'. There may be anything from one to three rows of purlins each side of the roof. Sometimes the bottom row is just above the eaves (*no. 100*). Cruck roofs often have only one or two rows and in base-cruck roofs there is a roof-plate like the arcade plate of an aisled building, with a similar function to a purlin but set on top of or into the tie (*fig. 19*). Roof-plates are normally plain, but at the Old Vicarage, Bremhill, they are moulded. Purlins are chamfered in good-quality roofs (*no. 101*), or sometimes even moulded. A feature worth recording is the way they are attached to the cruck or principal rafter. They may be trenched, as at Linfurlong, Rowde, rest on a splint (*fig. 6*), or be clasped inside the principal rafter. In the majority of cases, however, they are tenoned. The roof-plate at Fowlswick is clasped with an unusual birdsmouth joint (*fig. 19*).

Wind-braces

Between the trusses of the roof and joined to the purlins or roof-plate, medieval houses in Wiltshire usually have wind-braces. Only rarely does a complete set survive. Some may have been removed for later dormer windows or chimney stacks. They strengthened the roof longitudinally but were also used as a decorative device, and many different patterns are found (*fig. 22, nos. 100 and 102*). Some

No. 101 *Chamfered truss and purlins in the hall roof of the Priory, Kington St Michael.*

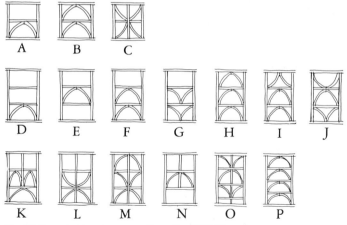

No. 100 *Wind-brace pattern in the roof of the lodging range at Brook Hall, Heywood, with a low, third row of purlins.*

Fig. 22 *Some wind-brace patterns used in medieval Wiltshire roofs.*

patterns occur with or without a third lower purlin. At Linfurlong, Rowde, the wind-braces are chamfered at the top and bottom. Wind-braces vary in size and curve depending on the distance between the purlins and the trusses. Sometimes they meet at the purlin and sometimes they are widely spaced. Usually they are fixed by a lap joint onto the backs of the purlins, but in early examples they may be tenoned in. Intermediate trusses of lighter construction were in use from the late fourteenth century onwards to form further compartments in the roof (*fig. 22*) type C, and most of the bottom row). At Bewley Court, the hall wind-braces are enriched with circles containing six-petalled flowers or tracery. Wind-braces are sometimes cusped, as at Cloatley Manor, Hankerton; Applegarth, Ogbourne St George (*no. 103*); and Axford Farm, Ramsbury (*no. 104*). At the Chantry, Mere, they are cusped in the hall (*no. 105*) but plain in the chambers over the service end. The hall wind-braces at Woodlands Manor, Mere, have foliage decorations at the tips of the cusps. There are a few houses that had cusped panels along the roof instead of wind-braces. One of these is South Wraxall Manor. Another was the Rogers' Manor (later called The Priory) at Bradford-on-Avon (*no. 106*).

No. 102 Wind-brace pattern at Talboys, Keevil.

No. 103 Cusped wind-braces and an arch-braced cruck truss at Applegarth, Ogbourne St George.

No. 104 *Cusped windbraces at Axford Farm, Ramsbury.*

No. 105 *Three tiers of cusped wind-braces in the hall roof of the Chantry, Mere. The end-walls of the room have collar and tie-beam trusses.*

No. 106 *Panelled roof of the 'Priory', the Rogers' manor at Bradford-on-Avon, before it was dismantled in 1937. The roof is in store and may be re-erected elsewhere.*

Suggested Further Reading

General and neighbouring counties

N.W. Alcock (ed) 'Cruck Construction: an Introduction and Catalogue' *CBA* 1981

M. Aston *et al* (ed) 'Rural Settlements of Medieval England' *Blackwell* 1989

M. Barley 'Houses and History' *Faber and Faber* 1986

J. Blair and N. Ramsay (eds) 'English Medieval Industries' *Hambledon Press* 1991 (for quarries, brickworks and timber)

R.W. Brunskill 'Timber Building in Britain' *Gollanz* 1985 (for terms and definitions)

R.W. Brunskill 'Illustrated Handbook of Vernacular Architecture' *Faber and Faber* 1987

J. Chapelot and R. Fossier 'The Village and House in the Middle Ages' *Batsford* 1985

G. Coppack 'Abbeys and Priories' *English Heritage/Batsford* 1990

Pamela Cunnington 'How Old is Your House' *Alphabets* 1981

Barbara Hutton 'Recording Standing Buildings' *Department of Archaeology and Pre history, University of Sheffield and Rescue* 1986

E. Lewis *et al* 'Medieval Hall Houses of the Winchester Area' *Winchester City Museum* 1988

D. Parsons *et al* 'Stone Quarrying and Building in England AD43–1525' *Phillimore* 1990

Porch to 65 The Close, Salisbury, the Abbot of Sherbourne's prebendal house. The porch was added to an earlier house in about 1475–1504. The archway to the right is not original.

N.J.G. Pounds 'The Medieval Castle in England and Wales' *CUP* 1990

L.A. Shuffrey 'The English Fireplace' 1912

J.T. Smith 'English Houses 1200–1800, the Hertfordshire Evidence' *HMSO* 1992

J. Warren 'Wealden Buildings' *Coach Publishing* 1990

D. Wilson 'Moated Sites' *Shire Archaeology* 1985

M. Wood 'The English Medieval House' *Phoenix* 1965 (the most useful general book)

Articles in the 'Proceedings of the Somerset Archaeological and Natural History Society', especially a series in Vols. 121, 123 and 125 on 'Base Crucks in Somerset' by E.H.D. Williams and R.G. Gilson.

Articles in Vernacular Architecture, especially on aisled halls (Vols. 6 and 17), four Somerset aisled trusses (Vol. 22) and medieval shops (Vol. 16).

Wiltshire

M. Aston 'Interpreting the Landscape' *Batsford* 1985 (contains many Wiltshire examples)

E. Crittall 'Victoria County History of Wiltshire' Vol. 4 *OUP* 1959

J. Haslam 'Wiltshire Towns' WANHS. 1976 (for early street plans)

T.B. James and A.M. Robinson 'Clarendon Palace' *Society of Antiquaries* 1988

N. Pevsner 'Wiltshire' *Penguin* 1963 (and later)

R.C.H.M.E. 'Salisbury' vol. 1 *HMSO* 1980 (covers the city and Old Sarum). 'Salisbury' vol. 2 (on the Cathedral and Close, to be published soon)

R.C.H.M.E. 'Churches of Southeast Wiltshire' *HMSO* 1987 (for comparison of doorway and window types especially)

Articles in 'Wiltshire Archaeological Magazine', 'Wiltshire Notes and Queries' and 'Country Life'.

To save space some architectural terms in this book have not been explained in full. The leader is advised to consult Brunskill 1987, Cunnington or Hutton in the list above.

Alterations to the gatehouse of South Wraxall Manor in about 1900, for the insertion of a two-storey bay window. The builders pose in groups with the tools of their trade. This picture illustrates how a roof could be supported while a side-wall was rebuilt. (fig. 12)

Places To Visit

Houses open at certain times: Great Chalfield Manor, Atworth (NT); Lacock Abbey, Lacock (NT); Westwood Manor, Westwood (NT); Sheldon Manor, Chippenham Without; Bewley Court, Lacock; 65 The Close, Salisbury (Salisbury and South Wiltshire Museum).

Inns, hotels, restaurants and tearooms: the Bell Hotel, Malmesbury; Bay Tree Restaurant (former George Inn), Salisbury; George and Dragon Inn, Potterne; Sign of the Angel Inn, Lacock; King John's Hunting Lodge, Lacock.

Shops in Salisbury: Beach's Bookshop, High Street; 8 and 9 Queen Street (china shop).

Octagonal pillar supporting the vaulted undercroft roof of the fourteenth-century guest house at Bradenstoke Priory, Lyneham.

End truss of cruck construction at 1 Ball Road, Pewsey. The wing at right angles, to the rear, is later.

Useful Addresses

Medieval Settlement Research Group, National Buildings Record, Fortress House, 23 Savile Row, London W1X 2JQ.

Society for the Protection of Ancient Buildings, 37 Spital Square, London E1 6DY (for pamphlets and advice on the repair of old buildings).

Vernacular Architecture Group. Asst. sec., Brick Field, 20 Kiln Lane, Betchworth, Surrey RH3 7LX.

Smoke-blackened hall roof at Lower Berrycourt Farm, Donhead St Mary, a grange of Shaftesbury Abbey. The truss has a cranked collar, chamfered arch-bracing and V-struts above the collar.

Cloately Manor, Hankerton. The wing to the left has a medieval roof (fig. 20). The manor was much altered in the late sixteenth century.

Acknowledgements

The Wiltshire Buildings Record is indebted to all those who have allowed their houses to be studied and recorded. The houses are mostly private and are not open to the public. Any requests for information about them should in the *first* instance be addressed to the Wiltshire Buildings Record.

We also thank Derek Parker and Dick Larden who prepared the photographs for publication, Colin Johns who redrew the plans, and Robin and Barbara Harvey who carried out additional historical research and made valuable comments on the text.

The photographs were taken by Norman Chapman, Peter Filtness, Robin Harvey, Julian Orbach, Barbara Rogers, Pam Slocombe, Alan Thomsett, Megan Watts, WCC Planning Design Group and Geoffrey Wright. Reproduction of the Buckler and Owen Carter drawings is by permission of the Wiltshire Archaeological and Natural History Society and *fig. 2* by permission of the Wiltshire Library and Museum Service.

The Wiltshire Buildings Record is an independent charity housed at the Library and Museum Service HQ, Bythesea Road, Trowbridge, Wiltshire BA14 8BS, tel. 0225 753641 Ext. 2718. It is open to the public on Tuesdays.

You can help the Record by allowing us to copy photographs, drawings and any other information you may have about Wiltshire buildings. You may wish to join and help to record buildings in your locality or draw our attention to threatened buildings which may be worth recording.

The Author

Pam Slocombe has had a life-long interest in all branches of archaeology and is a council member of the Wiltshire Archaeological and Natural History Society. She has extensive experience of studying local history through documentary research and was a founder of the Wiltshire Local History Forum in 1985. In 1979 she chaired the Steering Committee which set up the Wiltshire Buildings Record and she became and remains the group's part-time organiser. She lectures regularly on the work of the Wiltshire Buildings Record and was the author of the Record's first two books: *Wiltshire Farmhouses and Cottages 1500–1850*, and *Wiltshire Farm Buildings 1500–1900*.

Back cover: Old Abbey Farm at Stanley, one of the medieval abbey buildings later converted to a farmhouse.